U.S. $19.95
Can. $29.95

CRITICAL DECISIONS
Educational Development Curriculum

Earl B. King

Printed in the United States of America. All rights reserved under International Copyright Law. This book or parts thereof may not be reproduced in any form, stored in a retrieval system or transmitted in any form by any means – electronic, mechanical, photocopy, recording, or otherwise – without the express written permission of the author or the publisher.

CRITICAL DECSIONS
Educational Developent Curriculum

Earl B. King
ebking8@yahoo.com
Flossmoor, Illinois

Copyright © 2017
ISBN 978-1-943342-46-4

PublishAffordably.com
www.PublishAffordably.com | 773-783-2981

NARRATIVE
Critical Decisions

Newspaper headlines around the country have reflected gang violence and a failing, crumbling school systems as a national crises.

The Critical Decisions curriculum and research literature review study on gang solicitation was written to gain the attention of youth who are struggling in school and at home with low self-esteem and a lack of coping skills. At a press conference at The White House in 2011, Barack Obama asked, "Are we making those investments in those young people so that by the time they're eleven, twelve, thirteen, fourteen, fifteen ... they can make responsible choices because they feel they've got something at stake?"

U.S. Secretary of Housing and Urban Development, Dr. Ben Carson, spoke to a group of men and women at New Beginnings Church in Chicago during his 2016 presidential campaign. Dr. Carson spoke about his experience with gang violence growing up in Detroit, Michigan. He stated, "I saw people lying in the streets with bullet holes, the same type of things you see here in Chicago."

The Critical Decisions curriculum will provide the parent, the educator, or the trainer with the means to lecture students and young adults. The life development educational curriculum was written and designed for participants to demonstrate and recognize a problem situation. Then resolve the problem by utilizing good decision making-skills. These are proven techniques for students and young adults to have an impactful, positive outcome.

Earl B. King Chicago, Illinois

No Dope Express Foundation Celebrates 10th Anniversary
Chicago Symphony Orchestra - August 1998
Jet Magazine Article

▼ *Young Earl B. King II (l) introduces his father during the NDEF 10th anniversary celebration. NDEF member Robert Jones (c), who was shot and blinded by a stray bullet more than eight years ago, performs* The Greatest Love Of All *at the gala. LeAlan Jones (r), NDEF national spokesman, gives remarks at the affair. Jones is a Peabody winner and co-author of* Our America.

FOREWORD

We all live in a world that is undergoing significant social transformation. Despite having a more globally conscious human family in which language and racial differences are of decreasing importance, it is still important to acquire a variety of interdisciplinary skills and educational training to help improve one's quality of life.

I have known Earl King for many decades. He is a dedicated professional in the areas of life, literacy, and human development.

I am personally grateful that King decided to write this book to share his wisdom and vision concerning the effective steps to take toward attaining long-lasting life-development skills. As you read each chapter, King has outlined not only what to do, but also how to take each step that assures success.

In *Critical Decisions,* Earl King has made a timely and strategic contribution to helping all people understand the critical priority of acquiring life-development skills and the practical educational training that one needs to be successful in one's personal life journey.

King's literary and experienced genius is evidenced throughout his research literature review study on gang recruitment and this unique educational curriculum. I recommend *Critical Decisions* to all who want to fulfill their dreams and aspirations. Personal development is a process. It does not happen overnight. One of the amazing benefits of King's approach to life-development skills is that he presents the information in very achievable, practical personal actions.

In sum, *Critical Decisions* is an educational curriculum that everyone should read and use. In fact, you should pass this treasure on to others who will also benefit. Every life is precious, yet too often we miss opportunities to maximize all of our true potential. Through this remarkable writing, Earl King helps to make sure that these life-changing opportunities are not missed. Let's study together and become properly educated by a master educator.

Dr. Benjamin F. Chavis, Jr.
President / CEO
National Newspaper Publishers Association
Washington, DC

NOTES
EARL B. KING

God has always been the source of my strength, providing me with empowerment and respect. I want to express my gratitude to Dr. Benjamin F. Chavis, Jr., President and CEO of the National Newspaper Publishers Association and former National NAACP CEO, who has been a mentor and a true friend. He has opened doors of opportunity for me to explore new horizons. I appreciate his sincere and genuine compliments of my educational pursuits in his foreword for *Critical Decisions*.

I am well pleased to acknowledge and bestow the *Critical Decisions* Men of Honor awards to four men of dignity and unbending principle. The late Honorable John H. Stroger, Jr., the first African-American President of the Cook County, Illinois, Board of Commissioners, was a man who believed in America's finest values for all people, leaving no one behind. President Stroger provided healthcare, employment, economic development, and education opportunities for Cook County's 5.2 million residents.

The late Mr. Russell Lomax, Senior Vice President of Securities Properties Inc., was a man of fundamental principle. Mr. Lomax dedicated his life achievements to reaching out with his resources to help people who were left behind. Mr. Lomax served underclass Americans with dignity and grace.

Mr. Harold Dahlstrand is a man who believes that people should be treated respectfully regardless of their race, creed, or religion. Mr. Dahlstrand is a man who is not afraid to revolutionize without compromise when it comes to supporting those who are less fortunate. Mr. Dahlstrand's life has been one of caring and sharing, creating a better place for humankind.

Mr. Ernest Daurham, owner of the Daurham Corporation, is a man who leaves no rock unturned when it comes to spending his resources, time, and talent helping those less fortunate. Mr. Daurham's sponsorship and personal participation allowed many struggling not-for-profit agencies to keep their doors open to support youth by providing opportunities for their education and future dreams.

I am grateful to have experienced a mentoring relationship with these four magnificent men of honor. Without further ado, I am truly honored to receive the endorsement from Dr. Cornel West for *Critical Decisions*. Dr. West is a man who has been recognized as an educational freedom fighter for social justice, equality, and economic stability for those living in the shadows of poverty and hope.

Dr. Cornel West graduated as a National Scholar from Harvard University in three years. Dr. West is considered by scholars around the world as an American national treasure. Dr. West continues to beat the drums for empowerment and peace while supporting the pursuit of those who choose to make critical decisions to earn a quality education and a brighter future.

I want to take this moment to express my appreciation to Dr. Jayne R. Goode, who is a published communications scholar and Assistant Professor for the College of Arts and Sciences at Governors State University, University Park, Illinois. *Critical Decisions* began as a thesis I considered writing on gang solicitation while earning my master's degree in communication studies at Governors State University.

I registered for Communication 7110-01, Research Methods 1, Literature Review, and Study Design. I was overwhelmed by the support and encouragement I received from Dr. Goode. My educational relationship with Dr. Goode gave me an innovative and cutting-edge approach to researching the fresh, improved, revolutionary, and qualitative educational concepts that you will find in *Critical Decisions*.

I would be remiss if I did not recognize and give my extended appreciation to Professor Pamela Caddick, MA of Governors State University. Professor Caddick's class, Communication 8460-01: Communication Training, presented the opportunity for the success of my completion of *Critical Decisions's* life-development educational curriculum. Professor Caddick's educational labor of love throughout my final summer semester was the fruit of my new beginning.

I want to acknowledge three men who are dedicated servants of the No Dope Express Foundation (NDEF): the late Robert Storman, Ronald Damper, CEO of the Damron Corporation and Mayor Joseph Dupar of Calumet Park, Illinois. These are three honorable, trusted men of valor who have made critical decisions to help young people reach their ultimate dreams and educational pursuits.

No Dope Express Foundation Celebrates 10th Anniversary
Chicago Symphony Orchestra - August 1998
Jet Magazine Article

▲ *No Dope Express Foundation (NDEF) celebrated its 10th anniversary recently in Chicago. Earl B. King (r), founder-president-CEO of NDEF, extends warm wishes to (l-r) special guest, former New England Patriot football player Darryl Stingley, who was paralyzed while playing more than 10 years ago; Martin Luther King, III, president of the Southern Christian Leadership Conference, who was the event's keynote speaker; and Harold S. Dahlstrand, chairperson of Spiegel Group Inc., who was an award recipient at the gala.*

MEN OF HONOR

Honorable John H. Stroger Jr.
May 19, 1929–January 18, 2008
The First Democratic African American President of the Cook County, Illinois, Board of Commissioners

From 1994 until 2006 President John H. Stroger, Jr., was a champion for education, healthcare, and economic equality. In December 2002, his namesake John H. Stroger Jr. Hospital was opened with the leadership and dedicated healthcare services President Stroger provided to the 5.2 million residents of Cook County. President Stroger was a dedicated member of the Alpha Phi Alpha Fraternity, Inc., where he borrowed the expression, "A Vote less People Is A Hopeless People."

Russell Lomax
May 1, 1924–August 1, 1994
Board of Directors, No Dope Express Foundation 1989-1994

I want to acknowledge and give my overwhelming gratitude to the late Mr. Russell Lomax, Senior Vice President of Security Properties Inc., Seattle, Washington, and board member of the No Dope Express Foundation (NDEF).

Mr. Lomax paved the way for the NDEF program to have a national headquarters located at 1212 South Michigan, Chicago, Illinois, as well as the NDEF Educational Recreational Complex located at the Pullman Wheelworks Apartments at 901 East 103rd Street in Chicago, Illinois.

Mr. Lomax provided properties to housing programs for underserved inner- city Chicago youth to have the opportunity to showcase their educational skills and talents to become America's leaders of the twenty-first century. May Mr. Russell Lomax rest in peace.

Harold Dahlstrand
Board of Directors
No Dope Express Foundation, 1987-

NDEF is anti-drug, anti-crime, anti-gang, and anti-violence. It is a 501(c)3 not-for-profit organization, that is making critical decisions.

NDEF offers alternative life-development educational skills to remedy inappropriate decisions made by young teens and young adults. NDEF's philosophy is to reach youth at an early age to teach them to be aware of the pitfalls of economic and educational destruction that are caused by drugs, crime, and gang violence in underserved communities in Chicago.

Harold Dahlstrand has been a hands-on NDEF board member for over two decades, raising financial and educational resources to combat the grave challenges facing underserved communities in Chicago.

Harold Dahlstrand is Executive of Residence and Assistant Professor of Business at Elmhurst College (EC). He also heads up the Department of Business

Advisory Committee and is a full-time instructor of management and human resources. Additionally, he is the faculty advisor to the EC Department of Business Alumni Association and EC Student Human Resources Association and co-chairperson of the Department of Business's mentoring program.

Mr. Dahlstrand served as vice chairman of the board and chairperson to the office of the president of Spiegel, Inc., a $3-billion company that included the operating divisions of Spiegel Catalog, Newport News, Eddie Bauer, Distribution Fulfillment Services, and First Consumers National Bank. As the company's chief human resources officer, Mr. Dahlstrand managed human resource activities serving over 15,000 employees.

Harold Dahlstrand also served as one of America's finest: He is a Vietnam veteran.

Ernest Daurham
CEO of Daurham Corporation
Board of Directors
No Dope Express Foundation, 1984–

Ernest Daurham is the founder and inventor of Leisure Curl hair products and the first NDEF board member to sponsor twenty-five Chicago public schools with anti-drugs, anti-gangs, and anti-violence prevention and intervention programs. We have great respect for his countless contributions to not-for-profit agencies struggling to keep their doors open. Mr. Daurham is a firm believer of supporting communities services.

CRITICAL DECSIONS

Winning For The Children

Hyatt Regency Chicago - September 1990
NBA Legendary Great Hall of Fame Hopeful Bob "Butterbean" Love and
Former NBA Player Earl B. King Sign Autograph Basketballs at
Little City Foundation Charity Dinner

Endorsements

My name is Bob "Butterbean" Love, former American professional basketball player with the NBA's former world champion Chicago Bulls, and I now work as the Bulls' director of community affairs, speaking and reaching hundreds of thousands of youth and teens around the world.

It is with great pleasure that I give my personal support to Earl B. King and his Critical Decisions research study and also his outstanding life-development educational curriculum to teach our youth how to make appropriate decisions to become successful in today's society.

Earl and I have traveled around the globe encountering valuable experience that gives Earl a unique insight for educational goals and objectives. He has spent decades involved in the development and advancements of educational institutions at every level.

I am confident that King's Critical Decisions life-development educational curriculum will help transform the lives of those children who need it most.

Bob "Butterbean" Love
Chicago

My name is Michael W. Stuttley, former presiding judge of the Sixth Municipal District Juvenile Section of the Circuit Court of Cook County. I am writing in regard to Mr. Earl King. I have known Earl over thirty years. Earl King is a dedicated professional, having served as a valuable partner in many of my education initiatives extending over two decades. These initiatives were aimed as a service to benefit the youth population of the Chicagoland area, as well as to the benefit of the nation's youth population at large.

Earl King's *Critical Decisions* research literature review on gang solicitation and his unique life-development educational curriculum is a precious ingredient that our youth population is missing. King has served as executive director educational training specialist in addition to possessing extraordinary talents as a former professional athlete. Earl has a unique, keen ability to communicate effectively, counsel, and recruit a diverse population of people.

My views of Earl King are based not on what I think, but what I know. This is why I consider this work to be a blessing for all parents, educators, clergy, law enforcement, politicians, and social service agencies.

This life-skill educational training and gang research study will truly be a benefit to their agencies. I am certain it shall be a labor of love from Earl King, and the benefit to the youngsters and people will be priceless.

Honorable Michael W. Stuttley
Chicago

I am Gloster Richardson, former wide receiver and two-time American and National Football League Super Bowl champion of the Kansas City Chiefs and the Dallas Cowboys, respectively.

I salute Earl King for his vision to reach young teens by the masses with his long-overdue Critical Decisions research literature review study on gang solicitation as well his life-development skills curriculum.

Earl has been at the forefront of providing excellent educational and recreational-development training to young teens around the country. His workshops and seminars have helped teens to understand that decision-making skills are paramount in their future endeavors. He has demonstrated exemplified integrity, character, and professionalism while helping teens meet their educational goals.

His proven and unique one-on-one counseling has transformed youth who were involved in gang activity and making the wrong decisions. I have been a witness and can testify as to how Earl has mentored teens, instilling hope and providing opportunity for educational placement to enrich their life goals.

In addition, King has co-designed academic enrichment workshops and off-campus retreats with various local colleges and universities, while committed to his work by demonstrating his leadership skills to reach those less fortunate. Earl King is certainly a certified, experienced professional and educator.

Gloster Richardson
Chicago

The importance of Earl King's *Critical Decisions* research literature review study on gang solicitation and his life-development educational curriculum is a needed asset for those of us working in the field of African American men and boys.

Knowing how to make the right decisions as a young man is probably the most important skill they can have; it is a choice between life and death. Earl King is to be congratulated for creating this *Critical Decisions* life-development skills curriculum for educational learning and opening the doors of opportunity for those who are most vulnerable.

Bobby William Austin, PhD
Founder of The Village Foundation and National African Male Collaboration
Washington, DC

•

I would like to give high praise to Earl B. King for his relentless pursuit to educate us with his *Critical Decisions* research literature review on gang solicitation and his life-development educational curriculum that is so desperately needed at this time.

This timely, God-sent *Critical Decisions* educational curriculum could not have come soon enough to help guide and educate our youth to make the appropriate decisions in their lives. Critical Decisions lays out the blueprint for the remaking of the future of the thought process for the change needed to revitalize communities throughout America and abroad!

Rev. Dr. E. Ajamu Babalola
Founder of Ervin's All American Youth Club
Clearwater, Florida

Earl B. King has more than thirty years of sound expertise as it relates to introducing concepts modeled around cultivating and nurturing adolescents from at-risk backgrounds and gang solicitation. The innovative, experienced, and well-researched approach to developing critical assessments introduced in this educational life-development-skills curriculum will augment positive skill sets in at-risk adolescent populations.

In this digital age, Earl King has structured a disciplined and well-nuanced education lesson plan that engages and equips participants with the advanced life skills needed to succeed in their life endeavors. I learned from experience: I was one of his participants and a National Jr. Spokesperson for the No Dope Express Foundation (NDEF).

LeAlan Jones
Author and Peabody Award Winner of Our America
Chicago

•

Let me preface this letter by indicating that I have known Earl King for over thirty years and I am intimately familiar with his background and community and educational work.

I assisted Earl King in developing the No Dope Express Foundation from the ground up, so I was able to view the difference that the organization made in the lives of countless inner-city youth and their families. My experience as a criminal defense lawyer and a trainer of inner-city youth in transformational experiential programs since 1981 allows me to assess Critical Decisions from a unique perspective.

What I see is a deeply dedicated individual whose clear intention is to provide at-risk youth with the only type of learning that really makes a lasting difference. This learning is experiential in nature rather than informative. Putting a subject in a real-life situation where he is required to make a clear choice leaves an imprint on a person that rarely is forgotten.

Today's youth are given so many lectures and so much advice that most of it is invariably forgotten or at best taken for granted. With King's experience and real-life simulations, the participant will be able to have access to the process of decision making.

How do I make the right choice in a time of conflict and crisis? Do I look to the past for answers, or is it the future that I envision for myself that will inform my choice at this critical moment in my life?

Many of the people Earl King has worked with have good intentions. Such intentions, however, very often are insufficient to carry the day. Through experiential learning developed by those who "have been there," participants, in my opinion, will have a real chance to lead a successful and meaningful life one of purpose, commitment and passion.

Elliot R. Zinger
Criminal Defense Attorney
Chicago

•

My name is Harold "Noonie" Ward, former high-ranking Gangster Disciple. Making a critical decision has become a terrifying experience for youth looking for a way to survive.

Earl King has written a research literature review on gang solicitation as well a life-skills educational curriculum that will help change the lives of millions of misguided youth around the world. Critical Decisions will be a game changer in underserved neighborhoods and in our crumbling school systems giving our youth the opportunity to make life or death decisions.

According to national statistics reported in the Chicago Sun Times, the Chicago Defender, the New York Times, and the Los Angeles Times, black boys growing up in urban cities are less likely to reach the age of seventeen than non-black boys. I know firsthand and from experience that gang violence, drugs, and crime are major contributors.

These are real-life situations. I am eager and elated to support Earl King, who has been fighting the good fight while writing prevention curriculums and implementing alternative programs to combat drugs and gang violence. King's priority to help guide our youth to make the appropriate decisions will make the difference between them earning an education and becoming unemployed, incarcerated, or losing their lives on the street.

Harold "Noonie" Ward
Activist, Author, Film Director
Chicago

•

There is a major gap of life skills within a vast portion of today's youth. Young adults from a variety of upbringings will benefit from this model that provides a positive outlook and guidance.

Not restricted to underserved or underprivileged kids, this book targets widespread contemporary young adults that, due to technology's impact, struggle to deal with fundamental social skills and decision making. This learning experience will allow teens and twenty-something's to empower themselves where otherwise they would not have been enlightened.

In a positive light, the youth of today experience a lifestyle and culture that is constantly absorbing from the global network. Yet this opportunity simultaneously creates a platform for impending social issues and tensions to continue and evolve.

In spite of all of the Internet's remarkable opportunities for human growth and intellectual development, it has created an inescapable space for antagonizers to pursue their targets. As this is a contemporary issue lacking established problem-solving strategies, Earl B. King has provided a conductor to aid contemporary youth in their path of development through the twenty-first century's growth.

Itamar Amrany
Artist and COO
Rotblatt Amrany Studio
Chicago

FAMILY ACKNOWLEDGMENTS

I give thanks to God, and I acknowledge the remembrance of my mother, Mildred Richardson Barksdale King and father, John Barksdale, as well my sisters and brothers: Earlie King Brown, Shirley King Wallace, Willa King Green, Loraine King Beck, Elizabeth King Williams, Claude Barksdale, John Barksdale Jr., Theodore Barksdale, Percy Barksdale King, Ronald Denham, and to my aunts, uncles, nieces, nephews, and the entire family tree.

My parents nurtured and raised me to be respectful, accountable, and responsible. Their wisdom, encouragement, and teaching have always given me moral fortitude to earn a quality education, become gainfully employed and the patriarch of my family.

I want to acknowledge and show my respect in remembrance of my wife's family: my mother and father-in-law, Ozzie E. Smith and Ernestine Adell Campbell Smith, their daughters Darryll Smith King, Terri Smith Anderson and her husband and daughter William Anderson and Araka, and their son Rev. Dr. Ozzie E. Jr., and the late Barbara Westbrooks Smith and their children Lauran, Brian, and Dr. Ozzie E. III and to Jequetta Upton Smith, and their son young Westbrook Smith, as well as their families and the entire Smith and Campbell family tree.

I give a special thanks to my wife Darryll Smith King and our son Earl Barksdale King II.

Darryll, is an extraordinary wife and mother, always doing her due diligence and being a positive spirit. Darryll is a National Honors Society, Magna Cum Laude, and an Alpha Kappa Alpha (AKA) alumni of the University of Memphis, earning her Bachelor of Fine Arts in TV and Radio Broadcasting. Darryll has also been the recipient of an Honorary Doctor of Humanities.

Darryll is renowned around Chicago, as a radio and TV personality, as well as the co-chairman of the Board and Executive National Spokesperson of the No Dope Express Foundation (NDEF).

Earl King II is an exceptional son and young man, graduating from Homewood-Flossmoor High School with National Society Honors majoring in science. His scholastic excellence resulted in a four-year scholarship from Howard University, in Washington, D.C., where he excelled in his academics earning his Bachelor of Science Degree in Psychology.

Earl II is a proud member of the Phi Delta Epsilon International Medical Fraternity, D.C. Alpha Chapter.

Darryll and I were proud parents witnessing Earl graduate from Howard University at the top of his class as a National Collegiate Scholar, Deans List, and Magna Cum Laude recipient.

Earl II decided to teach school for a year at St. Ailbe

Catholic School and work for the Chicago Urban League. He explained his desire to teach and give back to youth growing up in the inner-city. We are proud parents to announce Earl recently accepted an offered of admissions to attend California State University, Fullerton, into their Clinical Psychology Master's Program.

I thank both of them for giving me the insight to write Critical Decisions, as well continue to accomplish my goals and always be there when I needed their supportive loving care. I am humble and grateful for the spiritual knowledge, guidance, and endorsement of our family's pastor and my brother-in-law, Rev. Dr. Ozzie E. Smith Jr., senior pastor of Covenant United Church of Christ in South Holland, Illinois.

▲ *Dr. Bobby William Austin (r), president and CEO of the Village Foundation in Alexandria, VA, is congratulated as an awardee by King and the gala's mistress of ceremonies, Chicago talk show host Darryl Smith-King.*

Bestowed Honor
Jet Magazine, August - 1998

CRITICAL DECSIONS

Keep Hope Alive
Former NDEF Board Member Michael Jordan
and NDEF Board Member Craig Hodges
Jet Magazine, May - 1990

▶ **Wish Fulfilled:** Robert Jones, a ten-year-old Chicago youth who was permanently blinded by a stray bullet at a city housing project, meets his hero, Chicago Bulls superstar Michael Jordan (left) at the Bulls' practice. Looking on (l-r) are Rev. T.L. Barrett, Raymond Fox, Jones' father, Bulls guard Craig Hodges, and Earl King and Sonny Parker, both from No Dope Express, a Chicago anti-drug organization, which sponsored the visit with Jordan, a member of the board.

Ex-NBAer Earl King's
'No Dope Express' Group
Teaches Kids To Shun Drugs
Jet Magazine, November - 1991

At news conference announcing renovation plans for center, King is joined by a group of Chicago children and (l-r) Larry Allen, manager, All Point Travel Agency; Elizabeth Williams, NDEF staff secretary; Christine Farmer, NDEF volunteer; and Dennis Holmes, NDEF vice president/general manager and head coach.

SPECIAL ACKNOWLEDGMENTS

In Beloved Memory of
Mr. Robert Lee Storman
"Stormy the Blade"

November 24, 1945-October 29, 2014
Public Relations and Spokesman-Thornton Township Communications Director and National Press Secretary for No Dope Express Foundation (NDEF).

Robert Storman life journey landed him public relations opportunities for the Chicago Defender, Ebony Magazine, the Chicago Urban League, the Nation of Islam, the Million Man March, and many of the largest African American churches in the greater Chicago area. He was affectionately called the "Blade" for the cutting, truths he told to effectively produce his public relations and marketing strategies. Mr. Storman also served as a Vietnam veteran.

No Dope Express Foundation Salutes Board Member Mayor Joseph Dupar Caumet Park, Illinois.

Honorable Mayor Joseph Dupar of Calumet Park, Illinois is recognized for his outstanding commitment fighting the good fight for justice, employment, education, and economic development.

Mayor Joseph Dupar is the first public official in the United States to rename a street in Calumet Park, Illinois on May 05, 2010 after US President Barack Hussein Obama II, the 44th president and first African American to hold the office.

On June 7, 2007, Mayor Joseph Dupar the Xerox Foundation, Xerox Community Involvement Program (XCIP), joined ranks with Cook County Board President, John H. Stroger Jr., and the No Dope Express Foundation (NDEF), and formed the Cook County Night Basketball League (CCNBL). Mayor Joseph Dupar is also a long standing board member of the No Dope Express Foundation.

The NDEF, XCIP, and the CCNBL, Life Skills Leadership Development Training Program provided a life development educational curriculum training for participants' progress educationally, economically, athletically, and physically. The relationships developed and created an olive branch to participants in underserved neighborhoods, assisting each participant in specific areas of their life. The activities provided the support to all participants to focus on education, economics, and healthcare goals.

Restoring Justice: (RIP) Laquan McDonald
The community is standing with newly elected Cook County State's Attorney Kim Foxx. She is the first African American woman to hold the second largest prosecutor's office in the country. Foxx was elected in 2016 after public outrage over the release of the video showing a white Chicago police officer shooting Laquan McDonald. McDonald, a 17-year old black teenager was shot 16 times. Laquan McDonald's death started a movement around the country against police brutality.

ACKNOWLEDGMENTS

First, I want to thank God for my brainchild Critical Decisions. This educational development curriculum will be a rewarding opportunity to reach millions of people to teach and educate them how to open the doors of success by making the appropriate decisions in life.

These initiatives help encourage me to write Critical Decisions.

I give a special thanks to an "Everyday Hero" the Honorable Cook County Judge, Michael W. Stuttley, for his endorsement and dedicated service to our youth residing in the Cook County Juvenile Detention Center, learning how to make the critical decisions to become law abiding taxpaying citizens in Chicago and across America.

When I think about law and justice, I think of Attorney Elliot R. Zinger, a founding board member of the No Dope Express Foundation (NDEF) and a true friend with deep compassion, always assuring the best results that life has to offer. I appreciate his endorsement of Critical Decisions and his countless hours of support as a NDEF Board member counseling and mentoring misguided youth in our community in Chicago and urban communities around the country.

A special thanks for Attorney Zinger's personal assistance to help produce a nationally broadcasted show to help stop the gang violence featuring NDEF and gang leaders around the country on the Oprah Winfrey Show. I also personally give my appreciation to Ms. Oprah Winfrey and her company for taking a bold stance to support a necessary initiative.

When I think of will power and intestinal fortitude, I think of a legendary man, Mr. Bob "Butterbean" Love, former Chicago Bulls superstar and now director of community affairs for the Chicago Bulls. Bob Love had a stuttering speech impediment his entire twelve years as a professional player. Love never was able to give a personal interview with reporters until he retired and had to work in corporate America.

The CEO of Nordstrom heard that Bob Love was working in Nordstrom's cafeteria. When he found out Bob had a speech impediment, he offered to pay for him to attend special classes to overcome this social dysfunction. I am proud that Mr. Love made the critical decisions to overcome his speech impediment to succeed. I thank Bob for his mentorship, endorsement, and inspiration in my life.

When I think of the heart of a lion, I think of my "cousin" a two-time Super Bowl champion with the Kansas City Chiefs and the Dallas Cowboys, Mr. Gloster Richardson. I appreciate his endorsement and his unwavering support as a role-model, coach, and mentor to serve our youth, traveling around the country playing in charitable golf tournaments helping to raise countless of dollars for educational scholarships.

It is not every day you meet a person like Harold "Noonie" Ward. Mr. Ward admits he made inappropriate decisions growing up in the Altgeld Gardens Public Housing Developments.

Harold "Noonie" Ward was a high-ranking Gangster Disciple. Mr. Ward was incarcerated before he decided to make the critical decision to turn his life around. He is currently an advocate, community activist, and the author of A Gangster with a Heart of Gold. Ward currently uses his life experiences to promote positive community programs for youth.

I appreciate the endorsement of Itamar Amrany, artist and COO of Rotblatt Amrany Studio, Chicago, Illinois. Itamar's is a person who is dedicated to make a difference in the lives of human development. I want to congratulate Itamar on his acceptance of admissions into the Master's Program in Emerging Technology and Design in Architecture, at the Architectural Association in London, England.

It is my sincere appreciation and respect for Dr. Bobby W. Austin, Founder of the National African American Male Collaboration (NAAMC), the W.K. Kellogg Foundation, Rev. Dr. E Ajamu Babalola, founder of the Ervin's All-America Youth Club, hip hop artist and music producer Robert Jones, a NDEF Jr. spokesperson who overcame being shot and blinded by a stray bullet when he was ten years old coming home from school in a gang crossfire, and LeAlan Jones, also a NDEF Jr. national spokesperson, political guru, author, and Peabody Award winner, for their endorsement of Critical Decisions.

I will forever cherish the No Dope Express Foundations

(NDEF), and Mr. Stedman Graham, author and founder of Athletes Against Drugs (AAD), collaboration with the National African American Male Collaboration (NAAMC), and our shared experiences in our groundbreaking innovative programs helping The National African American Male Collaboration become a success. This program was a collaboration of organizations making critical decisions enhancing educational opportunities in the lives of African American Boys and Men around the country raising $16.2 million dollars.

Earl B. King Speaker at
THE MILLION MAN MARCH
on Youth Development Education and Responsibility
Washington, DC - October 1995

I salute and appreciate all law enforcement agencies, lawmakers, and educators for protecting the rights of law-abiding citizens. I am extremely proud to have had the opportunity to work on an important historic initiative to stop gang violence and the killings in urban America as well the Million Man March with Dr. Benjamin Chavis Jr., former CEO of the NAACP; the Honorable Minister Louis Farrakhan and the Nation of Islam; the late Brother Carl Upchurch, founder of the National Council for Urban Peace and Justice Inc.; Mayor Emmanuel Cleaver, Kansas City, Mo; Rev. Mac

Charles Jones, senior pastor and host of the first Gang Peace Summit at St. Stephens Baptist Church, Kansas City, Mo; Prince Asiel Ben Israel, African Hebrew Israelite; the late Lu Palmer; Pastor Janette Wilson; Rev. Al Sampson, senior pastor of Mt. Fernwood United Methodist Church; Rev. Dr. Jeremiah Wright Jr., pastor emeritus of Trinity United Church of Christ, who led the charge and held a Gang Peace Initiative program at Trinity United Church of Christ; Rev. Harold Bailey, head of Probation Challenge, who held a Gang Peace Summit in Montego Bay, Jamaica; Father Michael L. Pfleger, senior pastor of Saint Sabina Church, who is always fighting in the streets for justice against gang violence; Rev. Dr. Ozzie E. Smith Jr., senior pastor of Covenant United Church of Christ, who always supported the NDEF program to eradicate drugs and gang violence; Dr. Cornel West; Willie Wilson, Entrepreneur and Philanthropist; Larry Huggins, Riteway-Huggins Construction Services; Inc.; Maywood police officer Grady Rivers Sr. Maywood, Illinois; Mayor Eric Kellogg of Harvey, Illinois; Alderman Julius Patterson of Harvey, Illinois; Mr. Zachary McDaniels of the Philanthropik Foundation Baltimore, MD; Bill Cosby; Larry "Big AL" Jordan from LA, Ca; the late Stokely Carmichael, NY; Rev. Dr. E. Ajamu Babalola, Clearwater, FL; Mayor Douglas H. Palmer, Trenton New Jersey; Brother Immanuel Shahid Ben Avraham, CEO of Life Skills Academy Inc., New Jersey; the late Omar Ali-Bey, and Khalid Samad, Co-Founders of "Peace In the Hood" Cleveland, Ohio; Rahim Jenkins, Washington, DC.; Maurice Perkins, Inner City Youth Foundation; Brother Sherif Willis, Harry "Spike" Moss, Uhuru Solutions, Minneapolis, Mi; Jim Brown Football Hall of Fame and Amer-I-Can Founder; and Activist Kublai K. M. Toure, Black Firefighters Association of Chicago; the late Marion Stamps; Rev. Dr. Jessie Jackson Sr. and the Rainbow Push Coalition; Rev. Al

Sharpton and the National Action Network; The Gang Nations; Brothers behind the Walls; the late Minister Fountain, Wallace "Gator" Bradley, author of Murder to Excellence and Executive Director of United for Peace Organization; Winndye Jenkins, 21st Century VOTE; Harold "Noonie" Ward activist and author of A "Gangster" with a Heart of Gold; activist Mark and Paul of "VOTE" West Side Chicago; activist Calvin "Omar" Johnson of the Work Ship Coalition; Brother Sherif from Minneapolis Minnesota; my cousin Bob Richardson; my niece and nephews Dawn Wallace, Arthur "Champ" Hill, Andre Nicholson, and Mark Barksdale Jr.

My personal gratitude and appreciation will always be a devotion of love and respect to the dedicated service of my late sister Mrs. Shirley Wallace, who was an honorable trustee and founding member of the No Dope Express Foundation (NDEF), in 1987. Her professionalism and beautiful spirit will always be cherished and remembered.

I want to express my gratitude to my sister Elizabeth "Liz" Williams, the honorable trustee of University Park, Illinois, for her unwavering endorsement and support for NDEF. Trustee Williams is a founding member of NDEF, and a valuable asset to the foundation. I also commend Trustee Williams, who is responsible for collaborating with community colleges providing a GED and higher educational programs for the University Park residents.

Many kudos for the support and endorsement from my nieces the late beautiful beloved Raquel A. Green and Rev. Dr. Chere'se Williams, the Will County Regional Board of Education honorable trustee, as well chairman of the planning commission for University Park and a lifelong national spokesperson for NDEF. Rev. Dr. Williams is the founder of the Lifting Them Up Foundation for battered women.

I am extremely thankful for my nephew Mr. Nathaniel E. Williams mentoring services as the NDEF music director. Mr. Williams teaching and patience with young teens wanting to become hip hop artists was always his gift for those less fortunate. I will always remember his mentoring and steadfast devotion to Robert Jones.

I commend and praise John Barksdale Jr., my big brother, for his endorsement as well his more than thirty years of labor and contribution as head of maintenance for the Chicago Housing Authority, helping those less fortunate make critical decisions while living in public housing.

It is with great respect I will never forget the service and tireless sweat and tears that Mr. Dennis B. Holmes, a founding member, vice president, program director, and head basketball coach of NDEF, for his decades of services mentoring young misguided youth to reach their dreams and educational pursuits.

I appreciate the services of Ms. Jimmie Etheridge, Vice President of Drug Prevention and Intervention for NDEF. Ms. Etheridge is a foot soldier who dedicated her valuable time and efforts in the war on drug abuse. Jimmie Etheridge endless contributions will never be duplicated and never will be forgotten.

A special thank you to the late Mr. Michael Washington, master state trooper for the Illinois State Police and director of law enforcement for NDEF for his dedicated lifelong services.

An extended appreciations goes out to NDEF board member Dr. Asr. Hapi, a naturopathic doctor who volunteered his services treating patients in underserved neighborhoods with holistic therapy.

Mr. Larry Williams Chicago, a State Farm owner and operator is another NDEF board member who always contributed to the cause helping young inner-city youth reach their dreams through NDEF educational programs.

A gracious appreciation goes out to Martin Luther King III, keynote speaker, and Mr. Henry Fogel of the Chicago Symphony Orchestra (CSO), for their sponsorship and support of the NDEF, Tenth-Year Anniversary at the CSO in Chicago.

I appreciate Michael Jordan for his support as a former NDEF board member of NDEF, especially his participation with Robert Jones and allowing inner-city youth to attend his Michael Jordan Basketball Camp at Elmhurst College in Elmhurst, Illinois.

My hat goes off to Craig Hodges, NBA three-point champion and NDEF board member for his lifelong support of children growing up in underserved neighborhoods.

The No Dope Express Foundation (NDEF), will forever be thankful to the late NDEF board member Daryl Stingley, former professional wide receiver for the New England Patriots, paralyzed in a game, and Kenneth Jennings, Simeon High School football player paralyzed in a game and NDEF Jr. Spokesperson for their courage's support and services to the youth trying to find a positive outcome in inner-city neighborhoods.

A heartfelt thank you goes out to Mr. Michael Dortch, Mr. Joseph "Jumping Joe" Pride, and Mr. David Britton for their hard work as the president of the NDEF gang and drug prevention chapter in Atlanta, Georgia, Philadelphia, Pennsylvania, and New York as well as to former NDEF board member Dominique Wilkins for his dedication to helping the less fortunate with their education and drug prevention pursuit.

I also extend my thanks to NDEF volunteer staff and board members, Mr. Ben Andrews; NDEF board member and former Harlem Globetrotters; Mr. Norman Davis, and the late Rene Brown, NDEF board members Chicago; Dr. Maria Coolican, University of Michigan, NDEF board member Ann Arbor, MI; Mr. Dale Robertson, and the late Mr. Dewayne Williams, NDEF press secretaries; Mr. Ron Booth, NDEF board member; Mr. Carl Carter, Mr. Michael Jennings, and Mr. Anthony Mealings, NDEF directors Chicago.

I give my admiration and praise to all of NDEF basketball participants and alumni: Maurice "Bo" Ellis, Phil the "Thrill" Harris, Marice "Ice" Culpepper, Lee Cummings, Terry Cummings, Mickey Johnson, the late Kevin Duckworth, the late Wayne Irving, Tony the "Levitator" Martin, Terry Bradley, actor of Hoop Dreams; Rickey Green, Alfredrick Hughes, Marlo Fenner, Juwan Howard, John "Big Dog" Robertson, the late actor Michael Clarke Duncan; Bo Rabb, Dennis J. Holmes, Jr., Jason Rooks Holmes, Christopher Parker, Lloyd Newman, co-author of Our America; NDEF Ambassadors: Darryll S. King, Jackie Rooks Holmes, and Lola Parker.

A special extended appreciation goes out to NDEF Cook County Night Basketball League champions 2008 sponsors, mentors, commissioners, coaches, administrators, high school, and college graduates, basketball alumni, and political officials: the late Cook County Board President John H. Stroger Jr; Cook County Board President Todd Stroger; Mayor Joseph Dupar, Calumet Park, Illinois; Commissioners: Bob Love, Gloster Richardson, Dr. Tommy Williams, Dennis B. Holmes, Leartha Arthur Scott, European basketball coach; Coaches: Steve Altman, Peter Nicholson, James "Skip" Robinson; Alumni players: Dave Altman, Jeremy Saffold, David Nicholson, Brandon Hayes, Chris Ross, the late Ivory Warmack, Jovon Andrews, Dave Caridine, Stan Bodley, Jordan King, Earl B. King II, Reo Logan, Robert Love, and Brody Love; Administrators: Darryll S. King, Emily Love, Claudia Bodley, and Tonya Cody Robinson.

Mr. Sonny Parker former NBA, Golden State Warrior, founder of the Sonny Parker Youth Foundation and former vice president of programs of NDEF, will always have a special place in my heart for his love and devotion to inspire those less fortunate to reach for the stars so that one day they may land on the moon.

I want to thank Mr. Marcelous Starks, former European professional basketball superstar and now a successful European professional sports agent for his endorsement and support. Mr. Starks one of Chicago's finest legendary high school alumni basketball players and a vice president for NDEF anti-drug and anti-violence programs worldwide, spreading the message to youth around the globe.

A special acknowledgement to Wallace "Gator" Bradley, the late Minister Fountain, Eddie Taylor, and Harold

"Noonie" Ward for their services as NDEF conflict resolution directors in Chicago, and urban America. Their contributions can never be enough to stop the violence in our communities.

I will never forget the heartfelt support of NDEF board members, Mr. Nick Celozzi Sr., and his son Joe Celozzi, for their donations and generosity sponsoring NDEF, with two new Chevrolet vans to transport thirteen young African American NDEF teens to the 1996 Olympics in Atlanta, Georgia. These NDEF teen members work their own hot dog and hamburger stands in Olympia Village, learning how to become entrepreneurs.

I was once told you save the best for last. I cannot say enough about the contributions of Robert "Stormy" Storman, who dedicated his talents and many skills to advance the cause to prevent crime, drugs, and gang violence in communities around the country. Mr. Storman used his press connections to get out the word to help stop the killings of innocent people in urban neighborhoods. His belief was that everyone should live a prosperous, healthy, and productive life. For our young children growing up in underserved communities, Robert "Stormy the Blade" Storman will be miss but never forgotten.

All of these wonderful people encouraged me to write Critical Decisions. I appreciate my family, friends, colleagues, and everyone who endorsed Critical Decisions and supported the No Dope Express Foundation (NDEF). Please forgive me if I left out anyone; it was not intentional. You all have my sincere heartfelt appreciation.

TABLE OF CONTENTS

Narrative i
Foreword iii
Notes v
Men of Honor ix
Endorsements xiii
Family Acknowledgments xxi
Special Acknowledgments xxv
Acknowledgments xxvii

Gang Solicitation 1
Black Gangs In Chicago 4
    Black Boys Joining Gangs 4
    Black Gangs 7
Gang Literature Review 9
    What Is A Gang? 10
    The Black Gang Culture And Theories 10
    Gangs Are Responsible For Social Problems 12
Research Analysis and Findings 17
    Methods 17
    Method Data Analysis 19
    Discussion And Findings 19

References 23

LIFE DEVELOPMENT EDUCATIONAL CURRICULUM 27
Risk-Taking Designed Simulation Situations 29
    Team Building 30
    Critical Thinking 30
    Decision Making 31
    Loyalty and Obedience 31
    Negotiation 32
    Nonverbal Communication 32
    Peer Pressure 33
    Persuasive Communication 33
    Conflict Resolution 34
    Coping Skills 34
    Risk Taking 35
    Self Discipline 36
    Social Interaction 37
    Verbal Communication 38
    Restorative Justice 39
    Topic/Discussion 40
Identifying Risk Factors 41
  Critical Decisions Teaching Guide 41
    Individual 41
    Peer 42
    Community 42
    School 43
    Family 43
  Protective Factors 44
    Peer 44
    Community 44
    Individual 44
    Family 45
    School 45

Background 46
　　　Target Population 46
　　　Target Population for Your Project 47
Training Needs Assessment 48
　　　Purpose: 48
　　　Criteria: 48
　　　Pro 48
　　　Con 49
　　　Life Skills Training Questionnaire 50
　　　Training Objectives 54
Training Workshop Outline With Timing 55

Training Development 62
Opening Exercises 64
Earl B. King 82

CRITICAL DECSIONS

National Gang Declaration
and Symbols
Chicago - 1993

Earl B. King and Jim Brown
National Report
Who Speaks For And To Young Inner-City Blacks?
Jet Magazine, June - 1992

Former pro football great Jim Brown (right) is an unquestioned champion of young men in the inner city, in part for his work with such groups as the Chicago-based No Dope Express, founded by Earl King.

GANG SOLICITATION
INTRODUCTION

Mobilizing a message to recruit African American gang members has been a social problem that has become a social phenomenon. It has been troubling to identify because it is an evolution for which researchers are trying to find concrete evidence to justify today's adolescent identity crisis. Chicago has been named the murder capital of the United States according to national statistics and media outlets.

President Barack Obama acknowledged Chicago's gang violence at his Gun and Gang Control Plan on Violence in American Cities conference at the White House on January 7, 2016. President Obama stated,

> "Children are stolen from families who never imagined that their loved one would be taken . . . by a bullet from a gun," he said, wiping away tears. "Every time I think about those kids, it gets me mad. And by the way, it happens on the streets of Chicago every day."

US Secretary of Education Arne Duncan and US Attorney General Eric Holder were sent to Chicago by President Barack Obama after the gang murder of Derrion Albert, a sixteen-year-old honors student walking home from Fenger High School in Chicago on

September 24, 2009. Secretary Duncan stated to the Chicago media,

> "This is not about money. Money alone will never solve this problem. It's about values, Duncan said. "It's about who we are as a society. And it's about taking responsibility for our young people, to teach them what they need to know to live side-by-side and deal with their differences without anger or violence."

Research scholars are interested in the sociocultural economics of the gang revolution and how to find a solution to prevent the violence in Chicago and other urban cities. To acquire this knowledge, researchers must know about childhood tendencies and predispositions that are used by gang members to solicit adolescents.

African American gangs have grown from being considered a block club socialization environment into a major social epidemic. The escalation of African American boys being targeted and solicited to join street gangs has become a communication nightmare in Chicago.

Malcolm W. Klein (1995) mentions and identifies how gang leaders continue to strategize plans to solicit black boys to become soldiers of gangs in urban America. Reliable sources and statistics provide awareness (Erikson, 1950) of how African American boys joining gangs at the early age of eleven to twenty years old are becoming neurotic not from frustration but from the loss of societal meaning in frustration.

Economic poverty, a failing educational system, incarceration, and injustice in urban cities are key reasons why African American boys are joining street gangs. This study will explain how communication strategies have become a phenomenon for gang solicitation. Chicago, Illinois has become one of the largest urban battle-grounds targeting and recruiting African American boys to join gangs.

James W. Glasgow (2007), the author of Gangs, mentions throughout his book the prominence of adolescents being solicited by criminal gang organizations. Glasgow, who is the state's attorney of Will County, Illinois, states that he wrote the book for parents' awareness, prevention, and intervention because of the growing population of criminal gang violence and recruitment throughout Will County and neighboring suburbs throughout Chicago, Illinois.

This study will also express how African American gang members continued to terrorize low-income communities and housing projects, causing destruction and violence throughout poor neighborhoods. There are two major Chicago street gangs this study will concentrate on: the Gangster Disciples and the Vice Lords.

The study will show how these two Chicago street gangs became major solicitors of young African American boys, focusing on their communications techniques and solicitation skills. This study will illustrate and provide qualitative information to communication scholars to understand how and why black boys are solicited to join these notorious street gangs in Chicago.

-One-
BLACK GANGS IN CHICAGO

BLACK BOYS JOINING GANGS
(Rationale)
Black gang leaders in Chicago are territorial. These leaders are extremely sophisticated in how they communicate to solicit new members. Their message is clear. Join or die in the mean streets of Chicago. This study will mention many poignant reasons why black boys join gangs.

Research will indicate the life path of gang solicitation. E. H. Erikson (1950), mentions, industry versus inferiority stage and earlier which expressed specifically how gang recruitment made members who were solicited enhanced their masculinity and intimidating reputation. This study will indicate the power struggle for false ownership in underclass communities in Chicago.

The Gangster Disciples control the South Side and the Vice Lords control the West Side. Both gangs recruiting members are giving a path to gain respect and opportunities for delinquency and negative behavior to make money and glorify violence. John W. C. Johnstone (1983), mentions gang recruitment was more prevalent among black adolescents in low-income depressed communities.

The erratic behavior of black boys being solicited to join gangs in Chicago, has created an identity crisis. Black gang members have higher interpersonal self-confidence and lower social self-confidence and would rather risk their chances selling drugs than attending school. The language they hear and understand is incarceration instead of education, especially in single parent households, without fathers. Chicago households are extremely vacant when you speak of fathers in underclass neighborhoods.

Research indicates this is a major reason why black boys become vulnerable to join gangs. Marie A. Bracki, Bonnie M. Dolson, and Kenneth Maurice (1997) comment about black fathers who were interviewed. The fathers recorded and spoke about their relationships with their sons.

Unfortunately, the fathers left at an early stage during their sons' preadolescent years. Government aid policy restricted many of these fathers or father figures from living in government housing and they proved to be ineffective, leaving these black boys with little hope and no guidance. Public housing enforced the policy and evicted any single female parent found guilty of housing a father figure or male companion in government housing.

My research will identify that black boys living in Chicago, are persuaded to join gangs as adolescents to sell drugs and commit crime because they are poor, uneducated, and unemployed living in depressed economic neighborhoods. (Brotherton, 1997). According to research articles and literature, gangs' delinquent practices are indicators of their existence.

Gangs are known to be traditional or cultural (Skolnick, 1995), controlled by territorial respect facing the defense of parochial community spaces (Suttles, 1968), "conflict-oriented" "retreatist" or "criminal" (Cloward and Ohlin,1960) depending on the opportunity structure, or "corporate" or "scavenger like" (Taylor, 1990).

The study mentions dealing in high volumes of drugs, illegal purchase of guns, and violence crossing territorial opposition in underclass communities. The research argues that black boys growing up in the inner-city in low-income housing without fathers to help raise them are seeking identity and recognition (Erikson, 1950). Once these black boys are recruited and accepted by the gang, they feel responsible.

The gang allows these boys to achieve a status that was impossible to reach outside of the gang structure. The research will indicate urban cities that are economically distressed are target areas for high gang solicitation. Gang protection is a key indicator of why black boys join gangs in urban cities where gang rivalry is strong and riddled with violence. Black boys feel safe and secure when they join a gang for protection.

Gang solicitation is accompanied by a mandatory commitment. The recruitment comes many times with threats and physical beatings. These beatings sometimes end with murder.

Black boys in poverty-stricken and underserved neighborhoods are seeking love, compassion, and acceptance. Earlier in the research indicates fathers or father figures left these boys when they were adolescents.

This was an emotional disorder, causing these boys to feel abandonment. Joining the gang gives these black boys what they are seeking most: brotherly love to fellowship and bond like a family. Gang functions are the extension these black boys are seeking trying to make up the void for growing up without a family structure.

BLACK GANGS
(Organization)
Gang intimidation, violence, drugs, murder, and racketeering have made Chicago unsafe, according to the article by the late Bishop Arthur M. Brazier (1969), whereas in this study the Woodlawn Organization located on the South side of Chicago was established since 1959. This agency is comprised of clergymen in the Greater Woodlawn Pastors' Alliance.

The alliance targeted unfair business practices, slum landlords, and the University of Chicago's urban renewal program of inadequate schools and facilities. Next they put in place a program for two of Chicago's most notorious street gangs. The Black P. Stone Nation, leader Jeff Fort, and the Black Gangster Disciples Nation, leader the late David Barksdale and former leader Larry Hoover. Jeff Fort and Larry Hoover are currently serving life sentences in the United States Penitentiary.

According to the Woodlawn Organization, T.W.O., plans were announced to create jobs for reformed gang members who were struggling to make ends meet.

This study continues to suggest that gang (E. H. Erikson,1950), mentions members who solicit new members are convincing, using psychology to control the minds of these adolescents to feel status in their neighborhoods by being a gang member.

According to The Chicago Crime Commission, "The Gang Book 2012" gave the statistic that Chicago has 100 street gangs and more gang members than any other city in the United States: 150,000.

There are other street gangs in Chicago that are known for their gang solicitations techniques, the Black Disciples, Four Corner Hustlers, Mickey Cobras, Latin Counts, and the King Cobras.

There have always been renegades. According to Malcolm W. Klein (1995), these are gangs known as copycats, cliques, and wannabe gang organizations involved in robberies, extortion, and stealing cars to survive. The Gangster Disciples and the Vice Lords strongly agree with intimidation in their initiation causing physical harm to the member being initiated.

One of their common initiation practices is five or ten gang members jumping on one recruited member for up to five minutes. Although the recruited member is allowed to defend himself, he is always outnumbered. Afterwards, they all hug and show love and lifelong companionship. Now the recruited member becomes official and must abide by the gang's rituals and governing rules.

-Two-
GANG LITERATURE REVIEW

The culture of why black boys are solicited by gangs and the structure of the gang organization and their presence has been a major challenge in Chicago. This literature review will analyze the theories on gang solicitation and the knowledge acquired from studies to develop gang reduction programs and communication strategies.

This topic is certainly debatable. Research will show the facts of this study are those of people and gang members who have lived this life experience. The study will provide accurate information from reliable sources for law enforcement, government officials, scholars, community leaders, and school administrators to review and use for their respective studies on gang solicitation.

The gang culture and theories of why single parent households are dysfunctional without father figures will provide communication scholars pertinent information to understand the value of fathers in the household. One of the important purposes of this literature review is to provide quality information on why black boys growing up in high populated underclass gang-infested neighborhoods are choosing incarceration instead of education.

WHAT IS A GANG?
A gang can be defined in four basic ways (Carl Upchurch and Earl King1993), according to the National Summit For Urban Peace And Justice report. According to Malcolm, W. Klein (1995), a gang is considered a group with a recognized leadership with less powerful members under command.

It is a structured organization with entities governed and supported by a submerged leadership. It is a membership group of individuals who are bonded with one another through good times and conflict. The gang or group usually merges with young member rather than adults. The gang or group's basic purpose is negative violent behavior submerging into a criminal enterprise.

There are many definitions to define the term "gang" whereas Klemp and North (2007) indicate that it is neither criminological research nor considered a part of law enforcement but are the complete opposite. The research indicates that gang culture is not affiliated with terrorist-type, hate groups and motorcycle gangs.

According to Webster et al. (2006), street gangs in this report offer skills and contacts the opportunity for crime and a means to illegal behavior into drugs, weaponry, and other illegal activity.

THE BLACK GANG CULTURE AND THEORIES
Huff (1998) recognized that violent behavior and criminal activity in underclass urban and suburban communities had a cultural effect connecting with juvenile delinquency and gang members committing serious crimes. Akers (1997), mentions differential association to associate a social learning process.

The theory is this learned behavior was acceptable causing violence and criminal activities in urban cities.

Hagedorn and Macon (1988) mentioned and made the distinction that groups of young black boys were juveniles working illegal activity in depressed low-income neighborhoods.

In Chicago, the Gangster Disciples and the Vice Lords controlled underclass neighborhoods surviving on government housing becoming drug lords and selling drugs to welfare residents. Poor Chicago, communities became drug-infested neighborhoods with no treatment for cure insight. Their gang solicitation was key in housing projects and underclass neighborhoods.

This study mentions how street gangs recruit and order their members to sell drugs, intimidate, and extort store owners to build their criminal enterprises. These are young black juveniles who feel they have been excluded from existing and becoming a part of today's mainstream occupation.

Research in Chicago, Milwaukee, Denver, and Los Angeles indicates that gangs are now becoming more apparent in their existing criminal activities. According to Thornberry (1998), hanging out with juvenile delinquents or at-risk peers are not proven reasons that boys join gangs.

However, close ties with gang members and connection with gang involvement is a key factor that boys join gangs (Thornberry, et al., 2003). Jankowski (1991) mentions that boys don't join gangs on their own as an independent decision, but they are solicited through a number of communication strategies residing in underclass neighborhoods.

Researchers have asked the question of the disposition of black boys who join gangs. An article by Stretesky and Pogrebin (2007) shows that youth who have criminal and violent behavior and have a disrespect of the law are prime candidates for joining gangs. Gang members are no different from one another in the social facilitation perspective until they become gang members. The enhancement prospective is the solicitation of new gang members who facilitate behavior in a criminal way and is not inferior and their violent tendency's increases once they become a member (Stretesky and Pogrebin 2007).

Out of all three studies this study indicated the enhancement perspective was most accurate in pinpointing why black boys join gangs.

The study illustrates the life path of gang members starting at the tender age of seven years old throughout their adolescence. Researchers mention how neuroticism in these underclass families are major causes of why black boys join gangs. Neuroticism is a personality trait that contributes to aggression, oppositional defiance, conduct disorder, and antisocial personality disorder throughout their adolescence and young adult years.

GANGS ARE RESPONSIBLE FOR SOCIAL PROBLEMS
Public housing in Chicago, Illinois has always been a social outcry for help or survival. Gang involvement and a high population of gang solicitation has been a major concern with law enforcement, government officials, Pastors and concerned citizens. Venkatesh, Sudhir, and Alladi (2001), mentioned researchers have stated that street gangs have always had an

entrepreneurial system in place.

The article by Bishop Brazier (1969) stated that gangs were sophisticated enough to realize making money in underclass neighborhoods in the ghetto was a means to survive. The gangs have always been a peer influence through socialization selling drugs and criminal activities to make money. Akers (1997) mentions the focus on differential association. Criminal behavior is a learned condition that young black juveniles in Chicago, have adapted through training exercises.

According to Drake and Cayton (1960), two researchers who believe in theory that gang members who were delinquent were also delinquent as a group resulting in delinquent criminal behavior (Curry and Spergel, 1990). Gang solicitation in the late 1960s, caught the attention of scholarly researchers who begin to monitor and evaluate gang activities in economically poor urban neighborhoods.

Chicago, became a focal point because of disenfranchised youth causing violent and criminal behavior in government housing. Political mobilization began to increase police presence thereby decreasing destruction of criminal activities.

Klein (1971) mentions gang solicitation and violent behavior along with criminal activities continued without an end in sight. The study indicated (Klein 1990) researchers concentrated on black boys who were disenfranchised living in public housing projects. They interviewed residents and were able to receive extensive reliable information to find out why there was so much criminal activity taking place. The following year in 1991, the study showed out of 118 young males who were documented living in public housing, 38 were active gang members.

The study revealed that gang solicitation and gang activity had a negative impact on adolescents living in poor public housing. The research concluded that gang activity was a major contributor in criminal behavior resulting in juvenile detention and incarceration. Klein (2000) mentions that parents were not in control of their family household, especially those without positive father figures.

Education became secondary to the criminal culture in these low income neighborhoods. According to the Office of Juvenile Justice Delinquency Probation (OJJDP), the prevalence rate of gang activity increased to 34.5 percent from 32.4 percent in 2008. At that time OJJDP stated that 167 cities that were a part of the 2009 National Youth Gang survey NYGS (2009), mentions a total of 1,017, gang-related homicides were reported.

OJJDP stated a 20 percent increase in gang solicitation and the population revealed a 5 percent increase. Steinberg, L. (1985), mentions in the development stages of adolescents between the age of 12 and 20, there is a change in the way they process their thinking and how they feel about themselves, leaving them vulnerable to negative and criminal behavior.

Research documents reported by OJJDP on black boys growing up in underclass neighborhoods in Chicago and other urban cities are more than likely to be uneducated, unemployed and members of a gang. Cohen (1955), states that when youth grow up in distressed disenfranchised communities, they are recruited by gangs to sell drugs and commit violence on others.

This line of criminal activity to them is considered to be part of the working class. Klein (1995) mentions research discovered in Chicago, and other urban cities black boys in their teens were experiencing psychosocial, biosocial, emotional, and cognitive changes leading down the path of violent and criminal behavior.

According to Berger (1994), youth have educational responsibilities once they reach middle school and peer culture becomes a major task that rewards sports and school activities that bring popularity. Sroufe et al., 1996 state that joining a gang becomes a psychosocial progression for some youth who are searching for alternative activities to gain popularity and status.

Researchers in this literature review are certain that gang recruitment, violence, selling drugs, and using illegal weaponry are causing Chicago's poor neighborhoods to continue down the road of disenfranchisement.

In 1990, shortly after a report came out on gang violence and drugs in Chicago public housing (Klein, 1990), Chicago Police Superintendent Martin called a press conference and stated his concerns of the rising gangs and drug epidemic in Chicago. Superintendent Martin, echoed loud and clear he was initiating a collaboration with the FBI, and the Illinois State Police to eradicate gangs and drugs.

Superintendent Martin sent a personal message to the Gangster Disciples and the Vice Lords street gangs stating the Chicago Police were the toughest gang in town. Throughout the years this collaboration of law enforcement has discovered through surveillance, undercover cops and stakeouts that these gangs are using modern technology such as Facebook, Twitter, and Instagram, etc., to communicate their criminal message. This study has reported reliable qualitative information that gangs, drugs, and alcohol played crucial roles in terrorizing underclass neighborhoods in Chicago.

The Gangster Disciples has a membership of over 50,000 members, and the Vice Lords has a membership reaching 35,000, as of the current date. According to, Toner (2013), reporter for the Chicago Sun Times, Superintendent Martin resigned in 1992 and never finished his task to stop gang solicitation, drugs or gang violence. Superintendent Martin died of a heart attack August 31, 2013, at the age of 84.

On May 21, 2016, over three decades later, Chicago's new police superintendent, Eddie Johnson, spoke to civic leaders and law enforcement officials about escalating gang violence and crime. According to Chicago Tribune's reporter Jeremy Gorner, Superintendent Johnson stated this was one of the most violent Memorial Day weekends in Chicago. Superintendent Johnson expressed his concerns by stating, "A gang culture that sinks its hooks into youngsters in Chicago's most dangerous neighborhoods almost at birth, so by the time they're 12, their destiny is set." He goes on to say, "It's either prison or death."

-Three-
RESEARCH, ANALYSIS AND FINDINGS

METHODS

This study will show why gang solicitation and socialization is a major element in the lives of young black males growing up in underclass communities in Chicago. Researchers will provide credible sources and literature on gang members while conducting personal qualitative interviews with individuals who are and were once gang members that will give a perspective of these violent methods of gang culture.

This research methodology report will allow communication scholars to understand how two gang leaders controlled and solicited gang members to patrol underclass neighborhoods in the city of Chicago. All names in the method report will be pseudonyms to protect the identity of the research respondents. In this study a review of gang literature was used to evaluate how current and former gang members were involved in the solicitation and socialization of gang recruitment.

Researchers will interview black males using a qualitative format in person with individuals who had and still have relationships, close ties, and interaction with gang members. The study will seek credible former and current gang members from the University of Chicago Criminal Justice Studies Department and

Chicago Gang History Project who have been perpetrators of gang recruitment and those who are willing to voice their opinions and testimonies of gang solicitation, and socialization.

The respondents in this study will include five current hardcore gang members between the ages of 11 through 20 years old. All gang members will be chosen based on their known identity as a gang member in the neighborhood where he has committed violence. They will be asked to engage and explain the structure of the criminal elements, mindset, and behavior of gang policy. Their testimony will include using gun violence on rival gang members in the community and being able to show physical gunshot body wounds perpetrated by rival gang members.

Each member will be chosen based on their testimony as a gang recruiter, using gun violence and selling drugs. The study will also focus on three educators from schools that are located in high populated gang territory. The educators will be chosen based on their educational background and a proven track record teaching education in underclass communities.

Last, this study will select three former gang members who are ex-offenders and two community activists that have strong ties and relationships with gang members. Using former gang members who are ex-offenders with hard-core criminal backgrounds and educators who teach in high gang populated underclass communities along with community activist will enhance the gang testimonies to be truthful.

This policy will secure qualitative interviews that enhance the understanding of this topic for communication scholars. All interviews will be semi-structure qualitative interviews on gang solicitation, criminal behavior, and gang socialization. Each interview will be in person and last about two or three hours.

Research volunteers, councilors, and educators will continue to provide qualitative experience and services at the No Dope Express Foundation (NDEF), located in Chicago, Illinois. The No Dope Express Foundation is a national Chicago, community-based program that provides alternatives to the lifestyle of drugs, crime, gangs, and life on the streets.

Through education, after school programs, retreats, sporting events, days at the beach, intervention and prevention programs, seminars, workshops, outpatient treatment, and literacy programs. The No Dope Express Foundation (NDEF) seeks to assist individuals and families on their road to recovery and on to a healthy and productive God-filled life.

Method Data Analysis

Research respondents, will be ask to volunteer and engage with researchers to conduct interviews that will be recorded on tape recorders. Each respondent, will be asked pertinent questions concerning gang solicitation and their affiliation with the gang.

All respondents will be allowed to speak truth to their own testimonies without interaction. Detailed questions will be presented for each respondent with regard to the subject matters being discussed.

Discussion And Findings

This study reflects on the vulnerability of adolescents during their childhood development growing up in a poor family structure before they become victims of gang solicitation. This study concludes that deterrence strategies and gang reduction programs will help prevent young African American males growing up in underclass communities from going down the path of gang solicitation.

This study will present evidence that adolescents were targeted and solicited at a young age to become gang members. The study will find that African American males between the age of 11 and 13 years old will be easier to train and be trustworthy to the gang's constitution and bylaws.

This study will reflect that young members would be loyal willing and able to dodge questions when faced with other gang rivals or law enforcement. Research will reflect older members or those already attending high school are more vulnerable to cooperate with law enforcement and not adhere to the gang constitution.

The study will research why older members who are recruited are not as loyal or experienced at an older age as the younger adolescents. Research will reflect that gang members who are recruited at an earlier age become grounded in their position. Once they reach their late teens and early 20s, they gain a reputation to respect.

This research method data will become extremely beneficial to measure the decades of gang solicitation, violence, and terror that has plagued urban underclass communities.

The National Summit For Urban Peace And Justice study report was conducted in 1993.

The discussions and findings raised concern among the researchers to ask gang participant to call a moratorium on gang violence in urban cities in the United States.

According to Neal Pollack (1995) author of *The Gang That Could Go Straight*, Larry Hoover, leader of the Gangster Disciples, had a meeting from prison with the Gangster Disciples directing members to turn violence into votes and reform their activities and name to Growth and Development.

Mr. Hoover's plan was for gang members to pursue education, economic development, and to use their vote for political change to make a positive difference in underserved communities.

Many political and law enforcement officials in Chicago did not agree with Mr. Hoover's proposal. However, national prominent members of the NAACP, the Nation of Islam, Rainbow Push Coalition, Black Hebrew Israelites, community social service agency leaders, pastors, business operators, educators, political officials, and some law enforcement representatives were willing to give this plan a chance.

This study will reflect that over twenty years later, President Donald Trump addressed Chicago's gang violence at his GOP fundraising event August 11, 2015, in Birch Run Michigan.

According to President Trump a lot of "gang members" in America, especially those in Chicago, Baltimore, and Ferguson, are illegal immigrants and, if he is elected president "they're going to be gone."

Weeks after the GOP candidates remarks Chicago's top police officer Superintendent Eddie Johnson made a statement at a news briefing to Mr. Trump, saying. "If you have a magic bullet to stop the violence anywhere, not just in Chicago but in America, then please, share it with us. "We'd be glad to take that information and stop this violence."

Chicago's Mayor Rahm Emanuel stated at a Chicago Town Hall meeting, "Our city is being torn apart by young men who have given up on themselves and their future."

ESPN held a town hall meeting August 25, 2016, in Chicago at a South Side YMCA. They addressed gun violence and the responsibility of professional athletes. The panel consists of professional sports journalist, players, scholars and community activist. Some of those in attendance were Chicago's NBA Hall of Famer Isiah Thomas, young Milwaukee Bucks superstar Chicago's Jabari Parker, Chicago Bulls Rajon Rondo, WNBA Chicago Sky Cappie Pondexter, and mother of Chicago's NBA superstar Dwyane Wade, Rev. Jolinda Wade.

This research literature review on gang solicitation will give an urgent response allowing scholars and stakeholders to commit research, resources, and concrete solutions.

Research scholars will review four strategic program recommendation initiatives from this study. Education, entrepreneur business loans, economic development, and on the job training placement. This research study initiative is open for discussion for contribution and collaboration partnerships.

REFERENCES

- ABC News Chris Bury, Kristina Wong, and Mary Bruce, Murder of Student Derrion Albert, Chicago (2009)
- Akers, R. L., (1997)
- Berger, K., (1994)
- Berman Mark, Washington Post, Superintendent Eddie Johnson (2016)
- Bracki, Marie A., Dolson, Bonnie M., Maurice, Kenneth, (1997)
- Brazier, Arthur M., (1969) Author
- Brotherton, David C., (1997)
- Bullington, Jonahan and Delgado Jennifer., (1987)
- Chicago Crime Commission, The Gang Book (2012)
- Chicago Tribune, (2013)
- Chicago Sun Times Editorial Mayor Rahm Emanuel (2016)
- Cloward, and Ohlin, (1960)
- Cohen, AK., (1955)
- Curry, David G., Spergel, Irving A., (1990)

- Erikson's EH., (1950)
- ESPN 's South Side Town Hall on Athletes and gun Violence (2016)
- Glassgow, James W., (2007)
- Hagedon and Macon (1988)
- Huff, (1998)
- Jankowski, SM., (1991)
- Johnstone, John W. C., (1983)
- Klein, Malcolm W., (1971)
- Klein, Malcolm W., (1990)
- Klein, Malcolm W., (1995)
- Klein, M, Maxson C., (2000)
- Klemp and North M., (2007)
- NBC 5's Trina Orlando, Obama on Gun Violence, (2016)
- NBC News Chicago, Gang Violence Donald Trump (2015)
- Newsone Kirsten West Savali, Obama Chicago Gang Violence, (2011)
- NYGS, (2009)
- Office of Juvenile Justice Delinquency Probation (OJJDP), (2009)
- Pollack Neal, Chicago Reader (1995)
- Skolnick, (1995)
- Sroufe et al., p. 179-180 (1996)
- Steinberg, L., (1985)
- Stretesky PB, and Pogrebin MR., (2007)
- Suttles, (1968)
- Taylor, 1990

- The Daily Beast.com, Glawe Justin, and Carson Ben, Dr., Press Conference (2015)
- Thornberry, TP., (1998)
- Thornberry, et., (2003)
- Upchurch, Carl and King Earl, National Summit For Urban Peace And Justice Report, (1993)
- University of Chicago (UIC), Criminal justice Studies Chicago Gang History Project
- Venkatesh, Sudhir Alladi., (2001)
- Webster et al., (2006)

CRITICAL DECSIONS

LIFE DEVELOPMENT EDUCATIONAL CURRICULUM

CRITICAL DECSIONS

-Four-
RISK-TAKING DESIGNED SIMULATION SITUATIONS

Most children and young teens from underserved communities suffer from low self-esteem and lack of coping skills. Educators and trainers will teach participants ages 12–18, the differences between positive and negative risk taking. To gain the attention of the class, the training will involve hardcore real-life events of gang members displaying inappropriate behavior leading to illiteracy, unemployment, incarceration, and death.

Displaying these real life situations, the trainer will begin group discussions regarding beneficial life skills training strategies. The trainer will invite a former gang member to speak to the group and dispel the myth that being a gang member equals failure.

The trainer will have lectures and group discussions explaining how cyber bullying, and using social media, inappropriately can cause negative situations. The trainer will demonstrate how participants can research different topics by using different resources, such as internet searches, blogs, news sources, and social media, etc., for impactful positive outcomes. The educator or trainer will lecture on how to recognize a problem situation as well as resolve it with good decision making skills and techniques.

TEAM BUILDING

Topic	Objectives and Outcomes	Discussion Questions
Being accepted or rejected by a group	Following group guidelines rules and procedures	Discuss skills that will support group acceptance
Responsibility in group Behavior	Applying responsible group behavior	Discuss the importance of responsible group behavior
Group decision making skills	Identify democratic skills in a group decision process	Discuss positive and negative disagreements within a group
A responsible group leader	Identify the characteristics of effective leadership in a group	Discuss different levels of leadership responsibilities
Levels of leadership responsibility	Identify leadership skills and responsibility	Discuss effective leadership skills within a group

CRITICAL THINKING

Topic	Objectives and Outcomes	Discussion Questions
Appropriate behavior during critical situations	Identify a critical situation	Discuss the importance of appropriate behavior
Important acts and factors that add to critical situations	Identify factors that are important in critical situations	Discuss the benefit of acts and factors in critical situations
How you feel and think or behave in a critical situation	Describe your thoughts, feelings and behavior when you experienced a critical situations	Discuss how you might react in a critical situation
Ways to deal or cope with critical situations	Developing effective coping skills in critical situations	Discuss effective ways to deal and cope with critical situations

CRITICAL DECSIONS

DECISION MAKING

Topic	Objectives and Outcomes	Discussion Questions
Decisions that affect your life	Explain the value of decision-making skills	Discuss how your decisions will make an impact on your life
Making appropriate decisions	Explain how decision-making skills affects your family	Discuss the importance of a good decision-making system
First step in decision making: Identify the problem	Identify problems that occur when making decisions	Discuss a problem you have experienced making decisions
Second step: Discover the choice	Identify choices between people who make decisions	Discuss the different choices that were selected
Third step: Consider the pros and cons	Identify the pros and cons of decision-making skills	Discuss the pros and cons you chose making your decisions
Fourth step: Make the correct choice	Express how you made the correct choice	Discuss your participation with others while making the correct choice
Final step: Evaluate the results	Explain how you concluded your decision was correct	Discuss how your participation within a group made the correct decision

LOYALTY AND OBEDIENCE

Topic	Objectives and Outcomes	Discussion Questions
Respected sources of advice	Describe the difference between your family's advice and your friends	Discuss the difference between your teachers advice and your co-workers
Different answers to problems	Describe the different answers you received to solve a problem when you consulted your friends and your family	Discuss the different answers you received from your classmates and your teachers to solve the same problem

NEGOTIATION

Topic	Objectives and Outcomes	Discussion Questions
State your views on negotiation	State your rationale on your views on negotiation	Discuss your views and rationale on negotiation
Different opinions on subjects and issues	What are your views on opinions and negative issues	Discuss a negative or positive subject and give your opinion
State your agreeable negotiation solution	Explain and implement your mutually agreeable solution	Discuss a positive and negotiable solution

NONVERBAL COMMUNICATION

Topic	Objectives and Outcomes	Discussion Questions
Using appropriate eye contact	Demonstrate knowledge of appropriate eye contact	Discuss how to use appropriate eye contact
Using signals and body language to get attention	Demonstrate body language to gain a person's attention	Discuss body language and signals people used to get attention
Using nonverbal cues and signals effectively	Describe how to use effective nonverbal cues	Discuss the positive effects and results when nonverbal cues are used correctly
Using nonverbal cues ineffectively	Describe the negative effects of misinterpreting nonverbal cues	Discuss the negative effects of not understanding nonverbal cues
Using nonverbal cues effectively	Demonstrate knowledge of the effective use of nonverbal cues	Discuss the effective use of nonverbal cues

CRITICAL DECSIONS

PEER PRESSURE

Topic	Objectives and Outcomes	Discussion Questions
Saying no	Describe different techniques for saying no	Discuss effective techniques to justify saying no
Pressure: Embarrassment	Describe the difference between embarrassment and pressure	Discuss your personal experience of being pressured or embarrassed
Pressure: Anger	Describe how anger can be defined as pressure	Discuss how a person's anger can be defined as pressure
Pressure: Making decisions	Explain how peer pressure causes unwanted pressure	Discuss personal experiences your peers caused you to make inappropriate decisions
Pressure: Attending school	Identify how peer pressure can lead to poor school attendance	Discuss how negative peer pressure causes teens to make inappropriate decisions

PERSUASIVE COMMUNICATION

Topic	Outcomes and Objectives	Discussion Questions
Ways to persuade or sway people	Identify three types of persuasion skills	Discuss three ways you can used these persuasion skills
Correct ways to persuade or sway someone	Describe appropriate persuasion skills used in a specific situation	Discuss the correct ways to persuade or sway someone
Using persuasion or swaying skills in relationships	Identify negative and positive persuasion skills used in relationships	Discuss why persuasion or swaying skills are used in relationships
Correct and incorrect methods of persuasion	Identify the effects of negative and positive persuasion skills	Discuss the positive and negative outcomes of persuasion
Consequences of positive and negative persuasion methods	Identify persuasion skills used to persuade others	Discuss positive outcomes when persuasion is used effectively

CRITICAL DECSIONS

CONFLICT RESOLUTION

Topic	Objectives and Outcomes	Discussion Questions
How to recognize and respond to a problem	Recognizing a problem and finding the solution	Discuss how to resolve a problematic situation
How a problem develops	Identify how negative peer pressure can lead to a problem	Discuss how negative peer pressure can develop into a problem
Your feelings when dealing with a problem	Describe your perspective and feelings when you are resolving a problem	Discuss your feelings of others in problem solving
Ways to prevent a problem	Identify alternatives for problem prevention	Discuss prevention methods for problematic situations
Appropriate and inappropriate responses to a problem	Distinguish appropriate and inappropriate behavior to resolve a problem	Discuss appropriate decision-making skills to resolve a problem
Making the right decision to resolve a problem	Develop an effective strategy to resolve a problem	Discuss effective decision-making strategies to resolve a problem

COPING SKILLS

Topic	Objectives and Outcomes	Discussion Questions
Reacting to bad news	Describe different ways people react to bad news	Discuss different reasons why people react to bad news
After denial	Describe different stages of denial that may occur	Discuss the different stages of denial
Dealing with death	Identify ways to deal with death	Discuss different ways people deal with death

CRITICAL DECSIONS

RISK TAKING

Topic	Objectives and Outcomes	Discussion Questions
Risk-taking situations and what may happen	Recognize risk-taking situations and their possible outcomes	Discuss the pros and cons of risk-taking situations
Positive reasons for taking-risks	Describe the positive impact of risk-taking	Discuss some positive reasons for taking risks
Negative impact of risk-taking	Describe the negative impact of risk-taking	Discuss an example of a risk-taking situation that would have negative results
When risk-taking is appropriate	Describe situations in which risk-taking is appropriate	Discuss when risk-taking is appropriate
When risk-taking is inappropriate	Describe situations in which risk-taking is inappropriate	Discuss when risk-taking is inappropriate
Response to risk-taking situations that lead to positive or negative outcomes	Identify appropriate responses to both positive and negative risk-taking outcomes	Discuss how you would respond to a positive or a negative risk-taking outcome
Appropriate risk-taking decisions	Describe appropriate decision-making strategies to risk-taking situations	Discuss decisions making strategies for appropriate risk-taking decisions

SELF-DISCIPLINE

Topic	Objectives and Outcomes	Discussion Questions
Self-control	Describe the meaning of self-control	Discuss some examples and the meaning of self-control
When self-control is not used	Identify and describe poor self-control skills	Discuss when people use poor self-control skills
Having self-control in a negative environment	Identify ways to avoid negative behavior	Discuss positive outcomes in a negative environment
Expressing your feelings	Distinguish between acceptable and unacceptable expressions of feelings	Discuss the difference between acceptable and unacceptable feelings
How people act when you express feelings appropriately and inappropriately	Identify the consequences of appropriate and inappropriate expressions of feelings	Discuss how people express their feelings to appropriate or inappropriate behavior
How people feel when you express your feelings appropriately and inappropriately	Identify appropriate verbalization of feelings	Discuss the negative or positive impact of how people feel when they are mislead
What happens to your body when you lose control of your feelings	Identify physiological changes that may occur when a person loses self-control	Discuss what happens to your body when you lose self-control of your feelings
Ways to control your feelings	Describe techniques to resist losing control	Discuss ways to stay in control of your feelings
Ways to stay in control of your feelings	Demonstrate knowledge of techniques to regain control	Discuss ways to regain control of your feelings
Ways to keep your self-control	Demonstrate techniques to maintain self-control	Discuss examples of how to maintain your self-control

CRITICAL DECSIONS

SOCIAL INTERACTION

Topic	Objectives and Outcomes	Discussion Questions
Your personal space and the space of others	Distinguish between your personal space and others	Discuss the difference between your personal space and others
The importance of personal space to you and to others	Determine why personal space is important to people	Discuss why personal space is important to you and to others
When personal space is respected or violated	Describe consequences when your personal space is respected or violated	Discuss what happens when your personal space is respected or violated
Approach gestures	Identify and describe various approach gestures	Discuss examples of approach gestures
Appropriate and inappropriate approach gestures	Distinguish between appropriate and inappropriate approach gestures	Discuss the difference between appropriate and inappropriate approach gestures
Using appropriate and inappropriate approach gestures	Describe the consequences of utilizing appropriate and inappropriate approach gestures	Discuss what happens when you use appropriate or inappropriate approach gestures
Emotional and social effects of substance abuse	Identify the emotional and social consequences of substance abuse	Discuss the emotional and social effects of substance abuse
Physical, financial, social, and emotional effects of sexual behavior	Identify the physical, financial, social, and emotional effects of sexual behavior	Discuss the physical, financial, social, and emotional effects of sexual behavior
Emotional effects of sexual harassment and abuse	Identify the emotional consequences of sexually exploitive behavior	Discuss the emotionally trauma that occurs due to sexual harassment or abuse
Socially Acceptable and Unacceptable Behaviors	Distinguish between socially acceptable and unacceptable behavior in response to different environments or situations	Discuss examples of socially acceptable and socially unacceptable behaviors

Verbal Communication

Topic	Objectives and Outcomes	Discussion Questions
Using questions, commands, and statements appropriately	Describe the positive effects of using questions, commands, and statements appropriately	Discuss ways to answer and use questions, commands, and statements appropriately
When questions, commands, and statements are used inappropriately	Describe the consequences of using questions commands and statements inappropriately	Discuss the consequences when questions, commands, and statements are used Inappropriately
Using questions to obtain information	Describe how to use questions appropriately to obtain information	Discuss how to use appropriate questions to obtain information
Using commands to obtain information	Describe how to use commands appropriately to obtain desires	Discuss examples of appropriate and inappropriate commands
Using statements to relay information to others	Tell if statements appropriately relay information	Discuss how to use statements appropriately to relay information
Using slang appropriately and inappropriately	Distinguish between situations where slang is appropriate or inappropriate	Discuss examples of slang words and advise when it is appropriate or inappropriate to use them
Talking with a group	Describe how to communicate effectively in group settings	Discuss effective communication skills to apply in group discussions
Relaying information	Describe how to relay information in a logical grammatical manner	Discuss how to give information in a clear and concise manner

RESTORATIVE JUSTICE

Topic	Objectives and Outcomes	Discussion Questions
Laws help you live in society	Describe how laws help you live in society	Discuss laws that give you the right to live in our society
Laws protect rights of the individual	Describe how laws protect the rights of the individual	Discuss and identify the laws that protect your individual rights
Criminal law: One person against the group	Describe a situation when one person is against a group	Discuss and identify a situation when one person is against the group
Civil law: One person against another	Describe a situation of two person's against one another	Discuss and identify a situation of two persons against one another
Court hearing and procedural rules	Describe some procedural rules that apply in a court hearing	Discuss a list of different procedural rules that are applied in a court hearing
Defense lawyer: Proves when a defendant is innocent	Describe the role of a defense lawyer	Discuss two situations when you believed a defense lawyer was right and when he was wrong
Prosecutor: Proves when a defendant is guilty	Describe the role of the prosecutor	Discuss two situations when you believed the prosecutor was right and when he was wrong

CRITICAL DECSIONS

Teacher or Trainer _____ **Grade** _____

Student's Name _____

Date _____

Topic/Discussion	**A**	**B**	**C**	**D**
Conflict Resolution				
Coping Skills				
Critical Thinking				
Decision-making				
Loyalty and Obedience				
Negotiation				
Nonverbal Communication				
Peer Pressure				
Persuasive Communication				
Restorative Justice				
Risk-taking				
Self-discipline				
Social Interaction				
Team Building				
Verbal Communication				

-Five-
IDENTIFYING RISK FACTORS

CRITICAL DECISIONS TEACHING GUIDE: TOBACCO, ALCOHOL, AND OTHER RISK FACTORS

IDENTIFYING RISK FACTORS, PROTECTIVE FACTORS, AND PROBLEM BEHAVIOR INDICATORS

PREDICT FUTURE RISKY BEHAVIORS BY YOUTH

Risk factors function in a cumulative fashion; that is, the greater the number of risk factors the greater the likelihood that youth will engage in delinquent or other risky behavior.

INDIVIDUAL

1. Antisocial behavior and alienation / delinquent beliefs / general delinquency involvement / drug dealing
2. Gun possession / illegal gun ownership / carrying
3. Teen parenthood
4. Favorable attitudes toward drug use / early onset of alcohol and other drug use
5. Early onset of aggression / violence
6. Intellectual and / or development disabilities

7. Victimization and exposure to violence
8. Poor refusal skills
9. Life stressors
10. Early sexual involvement
11. Mental disorder / mental health problem

Peer

1. Gang involvement / gang membership
2. Peer use / alcohol tobacco and other drug use
3. Association with delinquent / aggressive peers
4. Peer rejection

Community

1. Availability / use of alcohol tobacco and other drugs in neighborhood
2. Availability of firearms
3. High-crime neighborhood
4. Community instability
5. Low community attachment
6. Economic deprivation / poverty / residence in a disadvantaged neighborhood
7. Neighborhood youth in trouble
8. Feeling unsafe in the neighborhood
9. Social and physical disorder / disorganized neighborhood

SCHOOL

1. Low academic achievement
2. Negative attitude toward school / low bonding / low school attachment / commitment to school
3. Truancy / frequent absences
4. Suspension
5. Dropping out of school
6. Inadequate school climate / poorly organized and functioning schools / negative labeling by teachers
7. Identified as learning disabled
8. Frequent school transitions

FAMILY

1. Family history of problem behavior / parent criminality
2. Family management problems / poor parental supervision and / or monitoring
3. Poor family attachment / bonding
4. Child victimization and maltreatment
5. Pattern of high family conflict
6. Family violence
7. Having a young mother
8. Broken home
9. Sibling antisocial behavior
10. Family transitions
11. Parental use of physical punishment / harsh and / or erratic discipline practices

12. Low parent education level / illiteracy
13. Maternal depression

PROTECTIVE FACTORS
PROTECT YOUTH AGAINST DELINQUENCY AND SUBSTANCE ABUSE

PEER

1. Involvement with positive peer group activities and norms
2. Good relationship with peers
3. Parental approval of friends

COMMUNITY

1. Economically sustainable / stable communities
2. Safe and health-promoting environment / supportive law enforcement presence
3. Positive social norms
4. Opportunities and rewards for prosocial community involvement / availability of neighborhood resources
5. High community expectations
6. Neighborhood / social cohesion

INDIVIDUAL

1. Positive / resilient temperament
2. Religiosity / valuing involvement in organized religious activities

3. Social competencies and problem-solving skills
4. Perception of social support from adults and peers
5. Healthy sense of self
6. Positive expectations / optimism for the future
7. High expectations

FAMILY

1. Good relationships with parents / bonding or attachment to family
2. Opportunities and reward for prosocial family involvement
3. Having a stable family
4. High family expectations

SCHOOL

1. School motivation / positive attitude toward school
2. Student bonding and connectedness (attachment to teacher, belief, commitment)
3. Academic achievement / reading ability and mathematics skills
4. Opportunities and rewards for prosocial schools involvement
5. High-quality schools / clear standards and rules
6. High expectations of students
7. Presence and involvement of caring supportive adults

BACKGROUND

This Life Development Skills Educational Curriculum will be used to improve decision-making skills for youth and individuals who make poor decisions, and demonstrate negative behavior. Life Skills Training identifies risk factors, protective factors, and problem behavior. This Life Skills Training curriculum was selected to improve the lifestyles and economic opportunities for youth and young adults to empower themselves.

The description and presentation of life skills training is beneficial. Life Skills educators and trainers will instruct participants in educating, promoting, and using positive communication techniques. One of the communication techniques will be social media. Trainers will encourage and teach participants to use social media demonstrating positive outcomes.

The training presentation was selected because life skills are the foundation of a productive life. At the end of the training, participants will understand the responses to risk taking situations that lead to positive or negative communication outcomes. Participants will choose to make positives decisions while using social media, eliminating delinquent behavior.

TARGET POPULATION

Challenges or Problems Your Workshop Will Address
1. The challenges we will solve through our training will include bad decision making, negative behavior patterns, peer pressure, problem solving, and nonverbal communication.
2. The desired on the job training we would like to see

from our trainees are better decision making skills, improved problem solving, and better behavior.

3. Our concerns are increased gang recruitment, poor school attendance, lack of problem solving and overall lack of social skills.

TARGET POPULATION FOR YOUR PROJECT

1. The target population for the life skills training are youth ages 12–18. These youth are from underserved communities and more likely to be male minorities.

2. The participants who will be participating in the training are usually unemployed and undereducated. These participants have found it difficult to find meaningful employment and even more challenging to seek higher education.

3. The participants in this training will be underserved youth ages 12–18, and 80 percent will have come from broken homes. Some of the participants will have used drugs or are gang members. This life skills training is relevant to their knowledge, skills, and attitudes (KSAs) because this training is about improving their lives. The trainers will make sure in the recruitment initiation that the participants will be allowed to have an open discussion about the content and the topic of the training. The participants will have a concise and clear understanding that the workshop training will not be used to alienate or discriminate against them or their family.

4. The conditions that will affect participant participation in our training will be their attitudes and social interaction skills. They will learn and understand that your attitude affects your altitude determining how successful a person can become.

-Six-
TRAINING NEEDS ASSESSMENT

PURPOSE:
The designed needs assessment technique will be a questionnaire.

CRITERIA:
These are some of the needs assessment technique topics and learning outcomes / objectives / study questions the participants will receive on the questionnaire.

- Cooperation in Groups: Being accepted or rejected by a group following guidelines, and learning skills that will allow your acceptance by the group.
- Decision Making: Discuss life-changing decisions some of your friends may have made and talk about your decisions you have made, good or bad, that had a lasting effect.
- Interpersonal Relationships: Learning how to communicate to people, demonstrating knowledge and how to interact, without conflict

PRO
The questionnaire technique was selected to make sure all participants participate while identifying with the topic and discussion questions. This questionnaire should prove to be less intimidating to the youth, while

providing the trainer a resource document to measure written accountability.

Con
I realize all participants will not adapt to this questionnaire or give all true answers, especially since this will be a somewhat new experience. Some participants who have not been a part of a training program will have the opportunity to adjust and our trainers will work with them patiently to fill out the questionnaire. The goal is for youth ages 12-18, to overcome their learning barriers so they will have the chance to succeed.

CRITICAL DECSIONS

LIFE SKILLS TRAINING QUESTIONNAIRE
All Participants Must Fill Out This Questionnaire
"Please" Answer All Questions

Name _____

Address_____

Phone number _____

E-mail _____

Gender ☐ Female ☐ Male   Age_____

1. Do you believe in communication with people?
   ☐ Yes ☐ No

2. Who do you live with?
   ☐ Both parents   ☐ Single parent

3. How many sisters and brothers do you have?
   Please write how many
   Sisters (   )   Brothers (   )

   Are you attending school / what grade?
   Please write what grade
   ☐ Yes ☐ No   Grade (   )

4. How many people work in your household including yourself?
   (1) (2) (3) (4) (5)

5. Are you in a gang?
   ☐ Yes ☐ No

6. Have you ever been arrested?
   ☐ Yes ☐ No

7. Has someone in your family ever been arrested?
   ☐ Yes ☐ No

8. Do you make good decisions?
   ☐ Yes ☐ No

9. Do you obey the law?
   ☐ Yes ☐ No

10. Are you loyal?
    ☐ Yes ☐ No

11. Do you consider yourself to have good behavior?
    ☐ Yes ☐ No

12. Do you follow instructions from authority figures?
    ☐ Yes ☐ No

13. Do you own a gun?
    ☐ Yes ☐ No

14. Does someone in your family own a gun?
    ☐ Yes ☐ No

15. Have you ever been shot?
    ☐ Yes ☐ No

16. Do you know someone who has been shot?
    ☐ Yes ☐ No

17. Have you ever shot someone?
    ☐ Yes ☐ No

18. Do you believe in conflict resolution?
    ☐ Yes ☐ No

19. Do you believe in group discussions?
    ☐ Yes ☐ No

20. Have you ever been homeless?
    ☐ Yes ☐ No

21. Have you ever been bullied?
    ☐ Yes ☐ No

22. Have you ever bullied someone?
    ☐ Yes ☐ No

23. Do you value life?
    ☐ Yes ☐ No

24. Do you want to earn an education and become employed?
    ☐ Yes ☐ No

25. Do you want to get married and raise a family?
    ☐ Yes ☐ No

Please Answer These Two Discussion Questions.

1. Topic—Decision-Making: Write what you think makes a good decision-making system and explain what is needed to have a good decision making system. _____

    _____
    _____
    _____
    _____
    _____

2. Topic—Peer Pressure: Describe different techniques to say no, without feeling embarrassed or experiencing peer pressure. _____

_____
_____
_____
_____
_____

TRAINING GOAL
Students will learn a wide range of specially designed simulation situations to develop / improve their cognitive behavior, and social skills.

Training Objectives

YOUR WORKSHOP TOPIC Life Skills Training

YOUR LEARNING GOAL: Students will learn a wide range of specially designed simulation situations to develop and improve their cognitive behavior, and social skills.

Objective 1: TAXONOMY LEVEL: _____ Understanding _____

YOUR OBJECTIVE	ABCD PARTS
Giving a series of confrontational interactions, gang members will be able to identify gang violence at a 90% accuracy as measured by testing methods.	**AUDIENCE** Students
	BEHAVIOR will be able to identify gang violence
	CONDITION Given a series of confrontational interactions gang members
	DEGREE at a 90% accuracy as measured by testing methods

Objective 2: TAXONOMY LEVEL: _____ Applying _____

YOUR OBJECTIVE	ABCD PARTS
Given a real-world situational role-play based on bullying on Facebook, gang members will be able to apply workshop techniques to resolve the simulated real-world situations 90% of the time.	**AUDIENCE** Student
	BEHAVIOR will be able to apply workshop techniques to resolve the simulated real-world situations
	CONDITION Given a real-world situational role-play based on bullying in Facebook
	DEGREE 90% of the time

Objective 3: TAXONOMY LEVEL: _____ Evaluating _____

YOUR OBJECTIVE	ABCD PARTS
Given workshop scenarios, gang members will be able to examine and identify inappropriate behavior and relationships between youth and gang recruitment at a 90% accuracy, as measured by performance testing methods.	**AUDIENCE** Student
	BEHAVIOR will be able to examine and identify inappropriate behavior and relationships between youth and gang recruitment
	CONDITION Given workshop scenarios

-Seven-
TRAINING WORKSHOP OUTLINE WITH TIMING

I. **Opening Exercises**

II. **Training Purpose for Opening Exercises:** The trainer will introduce the training curriculum to the participants explaining how this training will affect their lives as it relates to negative / positive risk taking decisions. This section provides for participant introductions, review of Training Goal and Training Objectives. It includes activities that build interest in the entire course, introduces some of the major ideas of the first part of the program, and aids in group building and learning about the participants.

Module 1:
Introductions and Objectives Time: 40 minutes

The Life Skills Training is a five-hour teaching program that focuses on risk taking, coping skills, conflict resolution, and group interaction.

A. Introduction of presenter and topic: Earl B. King, Life Skills Training

   1. **Team Building:** Team Building is an exercise that promotes positive risk taking, group interaction, and character building.

   2. **On-the-Spot Assessment:** Once trainers evaluate the participants they will know and understand

the dangers and dilemmas that these participants face each day in urban communities.

B. **Review of Training Objectives:** Participants will engage in open discussions on all three Training Objectives.

III. **Building Blocks:** Training Purpose for Building Blocks: The trainer will encourage and teach participants to use social media demonstrating positive outcomes. The training participants will learn and understand the responses to risk-taking situations that lead to positive or negative choices. This section will include lecture and activities that both teach the basic knowledge and/or skills and explore participants' attitudes and feelings about the topic. It also involves participants by interspersing lecture presentations with opportunities for group participation.

Break 10 Minutes

Module 2:
How to Recognize Negative / Positive Risk Taking Situations. Time 40 minutes

A. **Understanding and Retention Strategies:** Opening summary on good and bad decision-making situations.

B. **Lecture:** The trainer will discuss how good decisions are made with people you trust such as family, friends, teachers, and law enforcement.

Lunch: 1 hour

IV. **Middle Activities:** Training Purpose for Middle Activities: This training activity will help participants get involved, being attentive and listening to the trainer to understand the lesson plan. It includes activities that help participants review the building blocks and introduces ideas to be covered at the next stage of the program.

Module 3:
Six Important Skills Time 40 minutes

   A. Lecture: The trainer will explain that listening and hearing are two different things

   B. Participants Involvement Strategies: Listening Role Group Activity

V. **Advance Skills:** Training Purpose for Advanced Skills: This section will review the concepts and skills presented in this outline with an opportunity to be applied in real life experiences with training workshop content. Trainers will teach participants the differences between positive and negative risk taking and how to apply positive applications to real-life situations.

Module 4:
A Visual Experience Time: 40 minutes

   A. Interest Building Strategies, Leadoff Story/Visual: You Tube video

   B. Workshop Training Questionnaire

   C. Lecture: Review of Questionnaire answers and discussion on social media problems and how to handle a problem that may have occurred because of information on the internet.

Module 5:
Demonstrating Risk Taking Time: 40 minutes

   A. Lecture: On critical situation involving risk taking and making appropriate decisions.

   B. Alternative Methods to Lecturing: Demonstration A group decision making demonstration to reinforce learning good decision-making skills.

C. **Experiential Learning Approach:** Role playing participants will role-play a risk-taking situation they were involved in showing whether the outcome positive or negative and how to develop good decision-making skills.

Break 10 Minutes

VI. **Closing Activity:** Training Purpose for Closing Activity: Closing activities will assist participants in testing and evaluating their knowledge and skill set through real life experiences and peer evaluations. It will also encourage them to apply these activities to new problems and on-the-job (or at home) situations.

Module 6:
Putting It All Together Time: 40 minutes

A. Applying Skills

1. **Lecture Reinforcement Strategies:** Press Conference: A final review takes place within the framework of a simulated press conference in which the trainees prepare questions that are submitted to the trainer for her or his response. This is a way of revisiting the main points of the lecture through the questions asked and adding anything that was missed.

B. Evaluation

1. **Knowledge Application Test:** The trainer will announce he will be giving participants a pre / post-test. The test will be correlated to the life skills lessons. This training activity lesson plan will help the trainer determine the participants understanding of the lesson topics.

2. **Evaluation Handout:** Post-Workshop Survey

TRAINING EVALUATION PLAN

All participants will be given an evaluating assessment questionnaire to complete on their trainer, training, and experience in the Life Skills Training Program. The questionnaire will be graded in five categories that the participants will check for their answer. Those categories are "Poor, Acceptable, Excellent, Yes, or No." If the participants would like to express their opinions, they can also write an essay to accompany their questionnaire. An example of evaluation questions is below.

PLEASE CHECK THE APPROPRIATE BOX BELOW

1. The trainer was clear and concise in teaching me the positives outcomes on risk taking behavior?

    ☐ Poor   ☐ Acceptable   ☐ Excellent

2. The trainer was clear and concise in teaching me the negative outcomes on risk taking behavior?

    ☐ Poor   ☐ Acceptable   ☐ Excellent

3. The trainer helped me develop / improve my social skills?

    ☐ Poor   ☐ Acceptable   ☐ Excellent

4. Did the trainer prepare you to recognize risk taking situations when using social media that would lead to positive or negative consequences?

    ☐ Poor   ☐ Acceptable   ☐ Excellent

5. Did the trainer have you engage with participants and encourage you to challenge others in a logical manner for an agreeable outcome?

    ☐ Poor   ☐ Acceptable   ☐ Excellent

6. Did the trainer meet your needs and expectations you were seeking?

   ☐ Yes   ☐ No

7. Did the training help you develop / improve your social skills?

   ☐ Yes   ☐ No

8. Do you think the training design helped you respond to negative risk taking behavior leading you to positive outcomes?

   ☐ Yes   ☐ No

9. During your training, did the trainer provide you with the necessary material or resources?

   ☐ Yes   ☐ No

10. Did the Life Skills Training meet your needs and expectations?

    ☐ Yes   ☐ No

Collected Data

The data collected from the participant's evaluation will be used to adjust future training if necessary. I have learned in my studies that qualitative data collected is priceless, especially in life skills training. This participant data will provide useful information for program trainers to understand the process behind the results and assess changes in participant's perceptions and their well-being. This type of qualitative information will be used to improve and strengthen the design quality of the training for a more accurate evaluation outcome.

CRITICAL DECSIONS

TRAINING DEVELOPMENT

CRITICAL DECSIONS

-Eight-
OPENING EXERCISES

TRAINING PURPOSE FOR OPENING EXERCISES:
The trainer will introduce the training curriculum to the participants explaining how this training will affect their lives as it relates to negative / positive risk taking decisions. This section provides for participant introductions, review of Training Goal and Training Objectives. It includes activities that build interest in the entire course, introduces some of the major ideas of the first **part of the program and aids in group building and learning about the participants.**

MODULE 1:
INTRODUCTIONS AND OBJECTIVES TIME: 40 MINUTES

The Life Skills Training is a five-hour teaching program that focuses on risk taking, coping skills, conflict resolution, and group interaction. Module 1 will begin with the introduction of the presenter and topic: Earl B. King, Life Skills Training

OPENING EXERCISE:
Team Building: Team Building is an exercise that promotes positive risk taking, group interaction and character building.

Summary:

I selected Team Building because in the work place or in gang territory, young people encounter peer pressure and risk taking to feel a part of the bigger group. The trainer will use counseling one-on-one techniques to obtain information. The participants will discuss some of their past experiences and the peer pressure young people face when living in urban communities. The participants will be motivated to participate in open and honest discussions with their peers and the trainer, releasing any tension that would be related to peer pressure. They will work in teams to identify the risk they face when they are not team players good or bad and will share their thoughts through skits or a dramatic presentation.

Administration

1. The trainer will facilitate an open discussion on peer pressure and risk taking with Do's and Don'ts.
2. After the discussion, the trainer will divide the participants into small groups.
3. The participants are instructed to work as a team to demonstrate the outcomes of their discussions through either one-on-one skits or a dramatic presentation.
4. All participants will vote on the best skit or dramatic presentation
5. Discuss the votes and the reason why the wining selection was a winner.

Do's and Don'ts

- Honor each other
- Respect a person's space
- Move and speak with total respect
- Don't speak without thinking first

ON-THE-SPOT ASSESSMENT:
Once trainers evaluate the participants they will know and understand the dangers and dilemmas that these participants face each day in urban communities.

SUMMARY:
I selected On-the-Spot Assessment because Life-Skill trainers will know and understand the dangers and dilemmas that these participants face each day in urban communities. Just walking home from school can be a life-or-death situation.

For this training model, we will utilize painting, drawing, and writing.

ADMINISTRATION:
1. The trainer will facilitate a major discussion on risk-taking and how taking risks sometimes changes situations.
2. After the discussion, the trainer will pass out papers and crayons and ask each participant to draw a picture that describes a risk they have taken.
3. Participants will then be asked to verbally explain their drawing and what it means to them.
4. Participants will be asked to write down what they experience from gangs and peer pressure.
5. Each participant will share their paper with another class member and have an open discussion without negativity on each of their papers.
6. The trainer will solicit comments and questions and will re-direct self-doubt with a focus on positive risk taking for good of the community.
7. Obtaining training participant participation: will be in subgroup discussions

Questions for the Class Discussion:
1. How can risk taking improve my life and my family?
2. Is it a bad or good risk to give information to the police if you know of a gang crime?
3. What can we expect to gain from this training?
4. What can I do now to help my other peers learn about the negative effects of peer pressure and gangs?

Review of Training Objectives:
Participants will engage in open discussions on all three training objectives.
1. Giving a series of confrontational interactions, gang members will be able to identify gang violence at a 90 percent accuracy as measured by testing methods.
2. Given real world situational role-plays based on bullying on Facebook, gang members will be able to apply workshop techniques to resolve the simulated real-world situations 90 percent of the time.
3. Given workshop scenarios, gang members will be able to examine and identify inappropriate behavior / relationships between youth and gang recruitment with 90 percent accuracy, as measured by performance testing methods.

•

Building Blocks
Training Purpose for Building Blocks: The trainer will encourage and teach participants to use social media demonstrating positive outcomes. The training participants will learn and understand the responses to risk-taking situations that lead to positive or negative choices. This section will include lecture and activities that both teach the basic knowledge and/or skills and

explore participants' attitudes and feelings about the topic. It also involves participants by interspersing lecture presentations with opportunities for group participation.

Break 10 Minutes

MODULE 2:
HOW TO RECOGNIZE NEGATIVE / POSITIVE RISK-TAKING SITUATIONS. TIME 40 MINUTES

Understanding and Retention Strategies: Opening summary on good and bad decision-making situations.

Activity Summary: The participants will be given a written summary on risk taking, conflict resolution, and problem solving. The summary will contain the lecture's major points and conclusions to help participants organize their listening. The lecture will reflect on life skills techniques that will help the participants gather information to make good decisions. This lecture will help improve the participant's communication skills before they make a bad decision. The lecture will explain to the participants that there are positive options they can choose before they make the wrong decision.

ADMINISTRATION:
1. The trainer will hand out a document displaying good and bad decision-making situations.
2. The trainer will discuss how good decisions are made with people you trust such as family, friends, teachers, and law enforcement.
3. The trainer will explain and answer participants questions on how to use search engines to research on the internet, and at your local library etc., for positive outcomes.

WRAP UP / CONCLUSION:
At the end of the lecture session, the trainer will have participants form into three groups. The groups will discuss the advantages and disadvantages of good decision making. The trainer will end with a discussion asking each participant to write a summary on how they are affected by risk-taking changes, positively and negatively. The trainer will explain that the group with the best completed answers will win and receive tickets to Six Flags.

Lecture:
The trainer will discuss how good decisions are made with people you trust such as family, friends, teachers, and law enforcement.

Hour Lunch

•

MIDDLE ACTIVITIES
Training Purpose for Middle Activities: This training activity will help participants get involved, being attentive, and listening to the trainer to understand the lesson plan. It includes activities that help participants review the building blocks and introduces ideas to be covered at the next stage of the program.

Module 3:
Six Important Skills Time 40 Minutes

Lecture:
The trainer will explain that listening and hearing are two different things.

Participant Involvement Strategies: Listening Role

Activity Summary:
The trainer will begin the session with the lecture on expected learning outcomes / objectives on risk taking situations. This life skill activity will help participants get involved and understand what will be presented in the lesson. The trainer will remind the participants to listen carefully and use these outcomes they learn as a study guide and to take notes.

ADMINISTRATION:

1. The trainer will ask the participants to form three groups and each group select a leader.

2. The trainer will whisper in each participant's leaders ear the same activity lesson plan.

3. The trainer will ask each group leader to discuss two positive reasons for risk-taking situations and two negative reasons for risk-taking situations using Facebook.

4. The trainer will ask the group participants to follow the directions of the activity lesson plan he whispered to their designated group leader.

5. The trainer will explain that listening and hearing are two different things.

6. The trainer will ask all three group leaders and their team to submit a written summary answering the questions that their leader explained to them.

7. The trainer will give group participants thirty minutes to study with their notes.

8. After the test, the trainer will have an open discussion with the participants about the activity.

Wrap up / Conclusion
The trainer will review the participants questions with

them and answer any questions. The trainer will explain that this exercise activity was to see and find out how well each participant listened and followed instructions. The trainer will announce he will be giving each participant a pre / post-test provided in their life skills training manual. The test will be correlated to the life skills lessons. This training activity lesson plan will help the trainer determine the participants understanding of the topic.

•

Advanced Knowledge and Skills
Training Purpose for Advanced Skills: This section will review the concepts and skills presented in this outline with an opportunity to be applied in real-life experiences with training workshop content. Trainers will teach participants the differences between positive and negative risk taking and how to apply positive applications to real-life situations.

Module 4:
A Visual Experience Time: 40 minutes

Interest Building Strategies:
Leadoff story or Interesting Visual (YouTube Video)

Activity Summary:
Most children and young teens from under served urban communities suffer from low self-esteem and lack of coping skills. Trainers will teach participants the differences between positive and negative risk taking. To gain the attention of the class the trainer will start off the session with a video illustrating the negative effects of gang violence. The video will show real-life events of gang members displaying inappropriate behavior leading to illiteracy, unemployment,

incarceration, and death.

Displaying these real-life situations, the trainer will begin group discussion regarding beneficial life skills training strategies. Although the video presentation will be hardcore, the trainer will invite a former gang member to speak to the group and dispel the myth gang member equals failure. The video will show how gang members had to serve time in jail because of the wrong decisions they made. After watching the video, group participants will discuss making the right decisions versus making the wrong decision. The participants will understand how making decisions can affect not only them, but also his / her family, friends, coworkers, employees / employers, etc. The video presentation and group discussion will cover and explain how cyber bullying, and using social media, inappropriately can cause negative situations. The video will also demonstrate how participants can research different topics by using different resources, such as internet searches, blogs, news sources, and social media, etc., for impactful positive outcomes.

Administration / Directions for Activity
1. Before the workshop training lecture session begins, the trainer will announce the viewing of a video presentation demonstrating the negative effects of gang violence.

2. The trainer will show the video and suggest that after the video the participants can engage and role play on making better choices.

3. At the conclusion of the video, role play, and discussion, the trainer will lead group discussions on critical situations involving risk taking and making good decisions.

"ROLE PLAY DEMONSTRATION"

- A participant will create a risk-taking situations that would cause him to be arrested and serve jail time similar to the one he saw on the video and ask participants to respond.
- Participant will state he and his friend are in a major department store.
- His friend will ask him to steal an expensive watch.
- He steals the watch, gets caught and is arrested.
- What decision would you have made?
- Then participants will sit down and have a group discussion.

Wrap up / Conclusion
After the role play and group discussion, the trainer will answer participant questions on risk taking behavior. The trainer will give a short lecture on how risk-taking is a topic that can also include non-verbal communication such as cyber bullying and social media harassment. The trainer will end the session explaining how the use of the internet and other resources can help a person make good decisions by providing correct facts into their argument.

The trainer distributes
the Workshop Training Questionnaire
for completion by the trainees

Lecture:
Review of answers and discussion on social media problems and how to handle a problem that may have occurred because of information on the internet.

Module 5:
Demonstrating Risk Taking Time: 40 minutes

Lecture:
On critical situations involving risk taking and making appropriate decisions.

Alternative Methods to Lecturing:
Demonstration A group decision-making demonstration to reinforce learning good decision-making skills.

Activity Summary:
The activity is a group decision making demonstration. The instructor will stay focused because these participants are known to display negative risk-taking techniques. The purpose of this activity exercise is learning good decision making skills.

Administration / Directions for Activity

1. The trainer will ask the participants in the group to take turns using a dictionary, or the internet to conduct a search for words that the group would consider to be negative.

2. The trainer will ask the participants to suggest different ways to search for words. When discussing each processes participants may also do a variety of searches.

3. Then the group will discuss the advantages and disadvantages of the different methods they performed to navigate the system for information and come to consensus on the method that worked the best for them.

Wrap up / Conclusion:
At the end of the activity, the trainer will ask the group what they learned about using social media and the internet that would be considered good decision making.

Experiential Learning Approach:
Role playing participants will role–play a risk-taking situation they were involved in, showing whether the

outcome positive or negative and how to develop good decision making skills.

Role Playing
Activity Summary: The trainer will lecture the participants on recognizing risk taking situations and the positive or negative outcomes. After the lecture, the trainer will ask participants to write about a risk-taking situation they were involved in and whether the outcome was positive or negative. The trainer will explain that these writings will be the basis for a role play that will allow the trainees to both experience certain feelings and practice certain skills.

Administration / Direction for Activity
The trainer will direct the participants to select a person out of their group to demonstrate a live role play of their risk taking experience. The participant selected will provide a list of decision-making steps from the lecture he will use for the role play and the outcome. The trainer will explain to participants that the purpose of the role play is to display real-life situations and learn how to develop good decision-making skills.

"Demonstration Role Play Steps / Outcomes"
- Discuss risk taking situations and what may happen?
- Give some positive reasons for taking a risk and some negative reasons for taking a risk.
- Discuss when risk taking is correct or appropriate and when it is incorrect or inappropriate.
- Describe the positive impact or the negative impact on risk-taking situations.
- Discuss how you might respond if the outcome is positive or negative.

Wrap up / Conclusion
The trainer will use this assignment on role play to engage the participant to develop and demonstrate their mastery of the skills they are learning. The trainer will also use the role-play exercise assignment to evaluate progress on participant participation. The trainer will end the lecture and activity explaining to the participants there are no good or bad answers to most of the assignments, but they will be evaluated on their ability to present information in a clear and logical manner.

10 Minute Break

•

CLOSING ACTIVITIES
Training Purpose for Closing Activity: Closing activities will assist participants in testing and evaluating their knowledge and skill set through real life experiences and peer evaluations. It will also encourage them to apply these activities to new problems and on-the-job (or at home) situations.

Module 6:
Putting It All Together
Time: 40 minutes

Applying Skills: Lecture Reinforcement Strategies: Press Conference
A final review takes place within the framework of a simulated press conference in which the trainees prepare questions that are submitted to the trainer for her or his response. This is a way of revisiting the main points of the lecture through the questions asked and adding anything that was missed.

Activity Summary:

The trainer will give a lecture to the participants with the main emphasis to help find alternatives strategies for inappropriate risk-taking behavior. To reinforce these strategies the trainer will describe situations when risk taking is appropriate with participants during the lecture. To end the session, the trainer will have a discussion on gang violence in urban communities. The trainer will ask the participants to agree on a strategy to hold a simulated press conference to explore alternative strategies to inappropriate risk-taking behavior and to reinforce what they have learned during the lecture.

•

ADMINISTRATION:

1. The trainer will ask participants to agree upon a strategy to hold a simulated press conference.
2. The press conference will address de-escalating gang violence by using alternative strategies to inappropriate risk taking behavior
3. Participants are divided into groups of four, and each group will poses a question to the trainer that will help to clarify the lecture presentation on using alternative strategies to inappropriate risk-taking behavior.
4. The trainer will suggest to the participants bring up hypothetical cases to incorporate into their questions.

Wrap up / Conclusion:

At the end of the press conference and lecture on describing situations when risk taking is appropriate, the trainer will ask the participants to write down / identify appropriate responses to both positive and negative risk taking outcomes that may occur after the press conference.

•

Evaluation
Knowledge Application Test: The trainer will announce he will be giving participants a pre / post-test. The test will be correlated to the life skills lessons. This training activity lesson plan will help the trainer determine the participants understanding of the lesson topics. The methods of assessment will match the taxonomy level of each objective.

CRITICAL DECSIONS

Assessment Methods for My Objectives by Taxonomy Level	
Objective 1: Taxonomy Level: Understanding	
My Objective	*Examples of Types of Assessments*
Giving a series of confrontational interactions, gang members will be able to identify gang violence at a 90% accuracy as measured by testing methods.	Papers, oral/written exam questions, problems, or homework assignments that require (oral or written): Summarizing readings, films, speeches, etc. Comparing or contrasting two or more theories, events, processes, etc. Classifying or categorizing cases, elements, events, etc. Paraphrasing documents or speeches Finding or identifying examples or illustrations of a concept, or principle
Objective 2: Taxonomy Level: Applying	
My Objective	*Examples of Types of Assessments*
Given a real-world situational role-play based on bullying on Facebook, gang members will be able to apply workshop techniques to resolve the simulated real-world situations 90% of the time.	Activities that require students to use procedures to solve or complete familiar or unfamiliar tasks may also require students to determine which procedure(s) are most appropriate for a given task. These activities might include labs, performances, problem sets, prototyping, or simulations.
Objective 3: Taxonomy Level: Evaluating	
My Objective	*Examples of Types of Assessments*
Given workshop scenarios, gang members will be able to examine and identify inappropriate behavior and relationships between youth and gang recruitment at a 90% accuracy as measured by performance testing methods.	A range of activities that require students to test, monitor, judge, or critique readings, performances, or products against established criteria or standards. These activities might include journals, diaries, critiques, problem sets, product reviews, and case studies.

TRAINEE FINAL EVALUATION (SUMMATIVE)

All participants will be given an evaluating assessment questionnaire to complete on their trainer, training, and experience in the Life Skills Training Program. The questionnaire will be graded in five categories that the participants will check for their answer. Those categories are "Poor, Acceptable, Excellent, Yes, or No." If the participants would like to express their opinions, they can also write an essay to accompany their questionnaire. An example of the evaluation is below.

Please Check
Poor-Acceptable-Execellent-Yes-Or-No-For- Answer

1. The trainer was clear and concise in teaching me the positives outcomes on risk taking behavior?

    ☐ Poor   ☐ Acceptable   ☐ Excellent

2. The trainer was clear and concise in teaching me the negative outcomes on risk taking behavior?

    ☐ Poor   ☐ Acceptable   ☐ Excellent

3. The trainer helped me develop / improve my social skills?

    ☐ Poor   ☐ Acceptable   ☐ Excellent

4. Did the trainer prepare you to recognize risk taking situations when using social media that would lead to positive or negative consequences?

    ☐ Poor   ☐ Acceptable   ☐ Excellent

5. Did the trainer have you engage with participants and encourage you to challenge others in a logical manner for an agreeable outcome?

    ☐ Poor   ☐ Acceptable   ☐ Excellent

6. Did the trainer meet your needs and expectations you were seeking?

   ❑ Yes   ❑ No

7. Did the training helped you develop / improve your social skills?

   ❑ Yes   ❑ No

8. Do you think the training design helped you respond to negative risk-taking behavior leading you to positive outcomes?

   ❑ Yes   ❑ No

9. During your training did the trainer provide you with the necessary material or resources?

   ❑ Yes   ❑ No

10. Did the Life skills training meet your needs and expectations?

    ❑ Yes   ❑ No

•

COLLECTED DATA

The data collected from the participant's evaluation will be used to adjust future training if necessary. I have learned in my studies that qualitative data collected is priceless, especially in life skills training. This participant data will provide useful information for program trainers to understand the process behind the results and assess changes in participant's perceptions and their well-being. This type of qualitative information will be used to improve and strengthen the design quality of the training for a more accurate evaluation outcome.

About The Author
EARL B. KING

Earl Barksdale King, a Chicago native, had a dream and special purpose in life to earn a quality education and become a leader to help those less fortunate.

Earl, a graduate of Morgan Park High School, and Chicago All-City First Team Basketball Player, also excelled in academics scoring a 26 composite score on the ACT. King earned a four-year basketball scholarship and attended the University of North Texas in Denton, Texas. King majored in Business Administration and became the first four-year letterman in over 22 years.

King was selected as a Honorable Mention All-Missouri Valley Conference Player. His most memorable highlights were when King scored 75points in three games in the Christmas Tournament in Tulsa, Oklahoma and a 36-point performance against Bradley University in front of a nationally televised audience his junior year.

After completing his collegiate and sports career at the University of North Texas, King helped prepare the 1976 Olympic Basketball Team. He then played against them with such stars as Bob "Butterbean" Love former NBA superstar with the Chicago Bulls and Quinn Buckner, an Olympic Gold Medal winner and NBA standout. King began his professional career in the NBA signing a free agent contract with the San Diego Clippers, the WBA Las Vegas Dealers, and the CBA Continental Basketball Association. He also traveled the world and played on a traveling team throughout Europe.

In 1987, God gave King a vision and thus, the No Dope Express Foundation (NDEF), was born. NDEF is an organization dedicated for youth to earn a quality education and dispel the ills of drugs, crime, and gang violence with a multi-networking concept to create world unity.

King is Chairman of the Board and Founder of the No Dope Express Foundation (NDEF).

King has been recognized as an "Everyday Hero," for his outstanding service to the African American community by the Illinois Secretary of State. King has received numerous awards for his dedication and leadership throughout the community including the NAACP National Community Service Award and the Drug Enforcement Administration Award.

In 1993–94, King joined forces with Dr. Benjamin Chavis Jr. former CEO of the NAACP, the Gang Nations, along with national leaders and ministers on a crusade to stop gang violence and killings in urban America.

King is a true leader in his community. He was named "Man of the Year" in 1994 for Dollar and Sense magazine. He also was the National Regional Marketing Director and a speaker at the Million Man March in Washington, D.C. in 1995.

King is a motivational speaker and conference leader for various schools, colleges, and organizations. Another highlight is when King took 13 young boys from the NDEF program to the 1996 Olympics in Atlanta, Georgia for 30 days. They learned independent living and entrepreneurial skills by working their own concession stands inside Olympic Village in Centennial Park. Today most are graduates from college working and becoming peer counselors and young leaders around the country.

Earl B. King has been featured in many major newspaper articles and Jet magazine on several occasions. While landing the cover of N'DIGO magazine, he was recognized for his accomplishments for NDEF and its success. King has been on many TV talk shows such as C-Span, CNN, Oprah, Geraldo Rivera, and a number of local and national radio talk shows.

Le Alan Jones a NDEF graduate and national spokespersons is co-author of Our America, earning a Peabody Award at age 17. Jones attended Florida State University for three years and finished at Barat College of DePaul University in Lake Forest, Illinois. Jones earned a Bachelor of Science Degree in Inter- discipline in Social Science. Our America is now a movie on SHOWTIME.

Earl B. King is extremely proud to be a founding member of the National African-American Male Collaboration (NAAMC), as well one of the first executive committee members. The NAAMC is comprised of 32 youth-service organizations nationwide.

The mission of the NAAMC, is to dispel the ills and negative behavior of black males in crisis. This collaboration was founded by Dr. Bobby William

Austin, former Grant Director with the W. K. Kellogg Foundation, which he funded with a $16.2 million dollar grant.

Earl B. King is a former spokesperson and deputy director of operations of the Cook County President's Office of Employment Training for the first African American and now deceased Honorable John H. Stroger Jr., President of the Cook County Board of Commissioners. The Board Presidents Office of Cook County serves over 5.2 million residents.

King also worked as a VP consultant for Diversity Inclusion Management and Marketing Operations for the Spiegel Catalog Group Corporation, where he worked closely with Harold S. Dahlstrand, Vice Chairman of the Board and Chairperson to the office of the president.

Earl B. King continued his education as a transfer student, earning his Bachelor of Arts Degree in Interdisciplinary Studies attending Governors State University. He graduated cum laude, making the Dean's List, and was a National Tau Sigma transfer student Academic Honor Society recipient. King earned his Master of Arts in Communication Studies / Media / Marketing / Management Training at Governors State University in University Park, Illinois.

King earned his Ph.D. in Alcohol, Tobacco, and Other Drugs Counseling from Gospel Ministry Outreach Theological Institute, Houston Texas.

King received his Leadership Business Certification at the University of Michigan Ross School of Business in Ann Arbor, Michigan and the Stephen Covey's Business Certification in The 7 Habits of Highly Effective People,

Salt Lake City, Utah.

King is a proud member of the prestigious organization Kappa Alpha Psi Fraternity Inc. The organization is known for its integrity being on the front line of leadership and always in the struggle to help those less fortunate, providing innovative initiatives for educational success.

Earl B. King is the author of Critical Decisions. King's passion is to help organizations achieve their objective goals with his academic knowledge, experience, and professional skills.

To contact Earl B. King
for speaking engagements or leadership training:
(708) 257-2885 • ebking8@yahoo.com